EXPLORING THE HISTORY
OF
LEE-ON-THE-SOLENT

EXPLORING THE HISTORY OF LEE-ON-THE-SOLENT

John W Green and Robin A Money

CHAPLIN BOOKS

www.chaplinbooks.co.uk

Copyright © John W Green and Robin A Money
First published in 2013 by Chaplin Books
Second impression September 2013

ISBN: 978-1-909183-30-8

A CIP catalogue record for this book is available from The British Library.

Design by Michael Walsh at The Better Book Company

Printed by Imprint Digital

Chaplin Books
1 Eliza Place
Gosport PO12 4UN
Tel: 023 9252 9020
www.chaplinbooks.co.uk

For Jean and Jo

Into my heart an air that kills
From yon far country blows:
What are those blue remembered hills,
What spires, what farms are those?
That is the land of lost content,
I see it shining plain,
The happy highways where I went
And cannot come again.

A E Housman (1859-1936)
A Shropshire Lad

CHAPTERS

Acknowledgements .... *i*

Preface .... *iii*

1	Before the Beginning 1
2	The Lee Family Robinson 9
3	Land Ahoy! 15
4	Starting from Scratch 18
5	Piering out to Sea 23
6	Making Tracks to Where the Rainbow Ends 31
7	One for the Road 44
8	Tradesmen's Entrance 52
9	Back to School 60
10	See you in Church 74
11	Staying the Night 82
12	Splashing Out 94
13	A Monument for All Time 97
14	Beside the Seaside – Beside the Sea 102
15	Cliffs and Butts 107
16	The True Story of Daedalus and Ariel 126
17	Seagulls over the Solent 145
18	On Cloud Nine 148
19	Blood, Toil, Tears and Sweat 155
20	When the Lights Came on Again 159
21	Middle Age Spread 161
22	Deviating from the Straight and Narrow 164

23	A Sight fit for a King	170
24	Sailing by	172
25	All Work and no Play	174
26	I'm a Celebrity… I like it Here!	186
27	We Will Remember Them	191
28	And Here's to You, Mr Robinson	198

Appendix 1 – Doomsday Book Entries	208
Appendix 2 – Town Time Line	212
Appendix 3 – Street and Road Names	215
Appendix 4 – The War Dead	220
Appendix 5 – The Robinson Family's other Development Projects	231
Appendix 6 – Maps and Plans	236

ACKNOWLEDGEMENTS

While the vast majority of this work is the result of our own joint research from a wide variety of documentary records within the public domain, we would like to record our thanks and appreciation to the following people in particular:

Malcolm Fare of the National Fencing Museum at Hanley Swan near Malvern for his efficient and generous help in providing the photograph of Charles Edmund Newton-Robinson and his team-mates at the 1906 Intercalated Olympic Games.

Evelyn Love, secretary of the Lee-on-the-Solent Women's Institute, for kindly allowing us access to the branch archives and comprehensive photographic records. Without her most friendly co-operation and enthusiasm in dealing with our request we would never have been able to include the all-too-brief account of the branch nor any of the splendid pictures relating thereto.

Bob Russell, secretary of the Lee-on-the-Solent Working Men's Club, for kindly giving up his time to meet with us to discuss the Club's history as well as taking the trouble to show us the Club's historic artefacts.

… and last, but by no means least, our long-suffering wives who have endured what must have seemed to have been an interminable period 'playing second fiddle' to our enthusiasm on the whole topic of this work. They have borne our absence from our otherwise normal domestic life both stoically and without the slightest complaint and to them this work is accordingly dedicated.

PREFACE

The Historic Walks along Lee seafront proved to be the catalyst that led to the inception, conception and eventual production of this account of the history of Lee-on-the-Solent.

It is intended to be as comprehensive and detailed as possible, using information from a wide field. Where this includes anecdotal accounts for which no supporting evidence has been found, the accounts have been included with a suitable caveat. A similar approach has been adopted in the cases where personal recollections have been included, hopefully without removing any of the humour or vibrancy of such memories.

Where monetary amounts have been quoted in the text, we have also endeavoured to provide a rough indication of each of those sums at 2013 values. The modern equivalents appear bracketed and in italics immediately after the historic figures, e.g. £334 *[£29,250]*.

The research for the writing of this account has been an exhilarating journey which has frequently been interspersed with spontaneous interjections of "I didn't know that". It is hoped that a similar experience will be enjoyed by those now embarking on exploring the history of Lee-on-the-Solent.

John W Green
Robin A Money

Lee-on-the-Solent
June 2013

❖ PARTICULARS. ❖

Lee-on-the-Solent Estate,

Of which the FREEHOLD BUILDING PLOTS now offered for Sale form part, has been laid out expressly as the site of a New SEASIDE WATERING PLACE, for which its Fine Beach, Magnificent Views of the Solent and Isle of Wight, dry gravelly soil and warm, though bracing climate, render it eminently adapted.

LEE-ON-THE-SOLENT FROM THE PIER.

The Estate is situated between Southsea and Southampton.

In the view it commands are the Towns of Cowes and Ryde, the ROYAL PALACE OF OSBORNE (immediately opposite) and the lake-like expanse of the Solent, the Finest Yachting Waters in the World.

A SPLENDID SEA BEACH, A GRAVEL SOIL AND SOUTHERN ASPECT,

Are among the natural advantages of the Site. The climate, though more bracing, closely resembles that of Bournemouth in warmth and dryness.

Excellent Bathing, Sea Fishing and Boating. Good School for Gentlemen's Sons.

I

BEFORE THE BEGINNING

During its past, Lee-on-the-Solent has had a pier, a railway linking it to Brockhurst where a connection to London was possible, hotels, boarding schools, a swimming pool, a cinema, a ballroom, and a tower. Unfortunately these did not all exist at the same time, otherwise it is quite likely that the town – with its prime location – could have become a premier seaside resort on the south coast. In an attempt to understand why this did not come about, let us go back to the beginning, or rather, before the beginning – to about 4000 BC.

In the early part of the twentieth century, evidence of a Stone Age settlement was discovered at Cherque. A large ancient refuse heap of shellfish shells was found buried together with knives fashioned from flakes of flint which were dated as being about 6,000 years old. As people of that era had no knowledge of agriculture or herding, any settlement would have been temporary and abandoned when the source of food ran out. Their dwellings would have been huts of mud and wattle and would have long since disappeared, leaving only the refuse heap and the stone implements as evidence of their existence. Unfortunately the significance of these archaeological discoveries was not appreciated at the time and they were removed in order to extract the gravel underneath. The resultant gravel-pit eventually became a refuse tip and is now, in all probability, covered by housing.

Because there were large deposits of gravel in the area, gravel digging became one of the area's major industries from about the eighteenth century. Underneath the few feet of gravel and brick earth that cover much of the Gosport Peninsula there is a layer of greyish clayey sand, known as the Bracklesham Beds, that contains some lignite and fossils, mainly of sharks' teeth. This geological layer was visible along some sections of the base of the cliffs at Lee-on-the-Solent before it was covered by the construction of the promenade in the 1960s. However it was still possible to find fossilised sharks' teeth in the shingle, especially at Elmore, until the late 1990s and before the beach was covered with aggregates dredged from the Solent.

Following the fall of the Roman Empire and the departure of the Roman army from the British Isles in 410 AD, there was a progressive breakdown of law and order and civilisation in general. The country became vulnerable to raids by Vikings and, in order to combat those incursions, towns and settlements enlisted the help of mercenaries of Angles and Saxons from what is now northern Germany. The arrangement with the mercenaries was that they could bring over their families and were paid in land which they were then at liberty to farm. Locally the Germanic influence is illustrated by the name of the track which, according to old maps, ran parallel to the coast from Stoce (Alverstoke) and across Brun Down (Browndown) and which was known as Easteran Weg, 'weg' and 'brun' being the German words for 'way' and 'brown'.

The incoming Anglo-Saxons eventually realised that they were more powerful than the people who had employed them and they gradually took over the running of the area themselves. The Anglo-Saxon Chronicle sets out details of the Anglo-Saxon history up to the time of the Norman Conquest. It records how the British Isles consisted of a number of kingdoms which were established after small fleets of three to five ships invaded various parts around the coast and seized the land of the Britons living there. In our local area it appears more likely that, rather than being taken over by invaders, the inhabitants were taken over by the people that they had invited here to defend them. There were two minor territories here, namely Wihtwara which means 'the people of Wiht' (the Isle of Wight) and Meonwara which means 'the people of the Meon' (the Meon Valley).

The mainland of our area remained pagan until 681 AD and the Isle of Wight until 683 when both were converted to Christianity with the arrival of St Wilfrid, the exiled Archbishop of York. However there was a tendency to declare conversion of an area when the local king agreed to be baptised, even if he failed to adopt Christian practices, and regardless of what the general population practised. This is illustrated by the fact that when churches were built they included pagan symbols in an attempt to appeal to the Anglo-Saxons.

The first historical reference to the Solent was in 686. The Venerable Bede, on a visit to the Isle of Wight, wrote: *The island is situated opposite the division between the South Saxons and the West Saxons being separated from it by a sea, three miles over, which is called Solente. In this narrow sea, the two tides of the ocean, which flow round Britain from the immense northern ocean, daily meet and oppose one another beyond the mouth of the river Homelea* [Hamble] ... *after this meeting and struggling together of the two seas, they return into the ocean from whence they come.* This double tide is one of the reasons why Southampton became a major port.

In the eighth and ninth centuries the Danes (Vikings) carried out regular raids on the British Isles and, in 865, their 'Great Heathen Army' landed in East Anglia and used it as a springboard for a lasting occupation with the result that, within ten years, they had taken over most of the rest of the country. Nearly all of the old kingdoms fell with the exception of Wessex. After an initial set-back, King Alfred built up an army and managed to defeat the Danes at the Battle of Edington in 878. Following a peace treaty Alfred transformed the kingdom of Wessex and put it on a permanent war footing and by the year 955 England was finally united under one ruler with a centralised government.

Let us now move forward to the most familiar of all historical dates, 1066, the Battle of Hastings and the ensuing Norman Conquest. Many of the noblemen of the victorious army were granted land by William the Conqueror and, by the time he died in 1087, some 92 percent of land was under Norman control. The population of England was just over two million and most of the cathedrals and abbeys had been demolished and replaced with Norman-style architecture.

One of the primary functions of the Doomsday Book in 1086 was to determine the tax to be levied on different communities. For the region where Lee-on-the-Solent now stands, within the four-mile coastal strip between the River Meon and the River Alver and extending about two miles inland, there are only four communities listed. They are Crofton (17 households) with 75 acres of farmland plus a church and a mill, Rowner (14 households) with 60 acres of farmland, Stubbington (9 households) with 45 acres of farmland, and Meon (2 households) with 15 acres of farmland. For other taxable assets and how they were measured see Appendix 1.

From this it can be seen that the area was very sparsely inhabited with only 42 dwellings whose occupants farmed just over 200 acres. That is only one twentieth of the land area of the six square miles (about 4,000 acres). Even though there were two larger neighbouring settlements at Titchfield (33 households) and Alverstoke (50 households), the whole area had a widely dispersed population.

On his death in 1087, William I was succeeded by his son William Rufus, who was not a popular ruler. He died in suspicious circumstances in a hunting accident in the New Forest in 1100 and was succeeded by Henry I, the fourth son of William I. Unlike his elder brother, Henry was popular. He ruled from 1100 to 1135, was the first Norman monarch to be fluent in English, and it is during his reign that we begin to see further signs of occupancy of our area. The name 'Lee', meaning 'clearing in a forest', appears in documents in many forms between 1133 and 1266 such as 'Leya', 'Lye', 'Lige', 'Ly' or 'Le'.

In 1132 the Cistercian order of monks founded the Abbey of our Lady of the Quarry (Quarr Abbey), a few miles to the west of the present-day Ryde, between Fishbourne and Binstead. The site became a valuable and productive property and, from the twelfth to the sixteenth centuries, stone from the quarry was used for religious and military buildings. Parts of the Tower of London were constructed of stone extracted from this quarry.

In 1133 (some 47 years after the Doomsday Book), Hamo Brito de Leya (the name strongly suggests that he was a Norman nobleman) granted part of his land at Cherc to the monks of Quarr Abbey. He also granted them toll-free passage for their ships along the seaboard that belonged to Cherc or Leya. This indicates that the lands of Cherque extended to the coast, and it would seem most likely that some of Hamo Brito's subjects must have lived somewhere along the coastline here to collect the tolls from passing and landing vessels.

In a charter, Gilbert le Brec of Cherc bound all of his men in Lye and Cherc to grind their corn at the mill of the monks. This was situated on land which they had as a gift from his ancestors in his fief of Cherc. He also granted and conceded to the monks, and to all who regularly made use of the mill, free access and regress through his land.

In 1186, John de Visor granted to the monks of Quarr his land between the Highway and the Moor, the farms Savarus and Ulrida, in his manor of Cherc. At this time, a Saxon track led from Ruwan Ora (Rowner) roughly parallel with and slightly east of the present Gomer Lane and Military Road. It then turned east near the present HMS Sultan main gate. He also granted them permission to berth their ships in his land free of toll and quietly and without the customary fees.

The Abbey of St Mary and St John the Evangelist was founded in Titchfield in 1232. The abbey owned many thousands of acres of land, had its own farm buildings and a series of fishponds. It would seem reasonable to assume that it was built with stone from Quarr Abbey which was probably transported across the Solent and up the River Meon. Documents suggest that there was quite a lot of traffic across the Solent from Quarr to Titchfield Haven at the mouth of the River Meon.

In 1236, the land belonged to Count Alan of Brittany, the tenancy at Lige is recorded as being held by Gilbert le Brec, and the great manor house with associated farms was probably located in the area of the present Manor Way. Another sub-tenant was Roger Markes who held the Manor Lee Markes.

An agreement was made in 1266 between the Abbot of Tichford (Titchfield) and the Abbot of Quarr regarding a tithe of the windmill which the Quarr monks had at Cherc. The agreement indicates that, although Hamo Brita de Leya, for the salvation of his soul and that of his wife's (Juliana), had given as perpetual and pure alms to the Abbey of Quarr the land on which the monks had built the windmill, the ownership of the land had now passed to the Abbey at Titchfield. As the agreement between the two abbeys was an amicable one it suggests that the Bishop of Winchester had considered Hamo Brita de Leya's gift to have been a gift to the Church and, as such, was in the care of the parish of Titchfield. This does, however, conflict with the fact that, in documents of 1554, a grange and farm at Cherc are recorded as being in the parish of Rowner. Possibly parish boundaries were redrawn at the dissolution of the monasteries.

The actual site of the mill is unknown. In *The Story of Gosport* written in 1966 by L F White, when referring to an early Grange farmhouse, he writes: *Adjacent to it and marked on the 6in. map stands a scheduled antiquity, Windmill Mound, formerly supposed to mark the site of the mill at Chark where the monks of Quarr Abbey were permitted to grind their corn. Recent research has shown that this is not so and that the mound was a defensive strong-point; it has been re-named on the latest map as Castle Mound.*

It does seem remarkable that this was not the original site of the mill, looking at it from the point of view of the monks of Quarr Abbey. They had a quarry on the Isle of Wight quite close to the foreshore of the Solent. If they had approached Hamo Brito de Leya asking for a site on the mainland on which to build a mill, they would have wanted a location not immediately on the coast, for security reasons, but a little way inland. Half a mile from the mouth of the River Alver, and adjacent to the river, there was an elevated position. This would have been ideal because the River Alver was directly across the Solent from their abbey. Water would have been the easiest means of transporting the material to build the windmill from the quarry to the mill site with a limited amount of transporting the heavy quarry stones over land.

Moving forward again nearly three hundred years, we arrive at the next recorded change of ownership. Between 1536 and 1541 Thomas Wriothesley (1505-1550), one of Henry VIII's principal secretaries, was involved in implementing the dissolution of the monasteries for which he was richly rewarded. He was granted extensive lands including 11 manors and 5,000 acres surrounding Titchfield Abbey in 1537 and immediately set about having the abbey converted into a grand new courtyard residence, using many of the monastic buildings, which became known as Place House. It seems that church conversions are nothing new!

Within the lands granted to Thomas Wriothesley were the rights to the water mill at Botley and also the rights to the manor of Lee Britten. In 1544 he became Baron Wriothesley of Titchfield as well as Lord Chancellor and in 1547 he was made first Earl of Southampton. 'Le Breton', an Elizabethan period cottage in Manor Way and the oldest house in Lee, dates from around this era. It is thought to be a smaller replacement home for the family when the great manor house was badly damaged by fire. As Thomas Wriothesley had also acquired the water mill at Botley, it makes one speculate that, if he did not need the mill at Cherque, did he have it demolished and then use the material to turn the site into a defensive stronghold?

The ownership of the Titchfield Estates, on part of which Lee-on-the-Solent was later established, passed through successive Earls of Southampton and then through female descendants until 1741. The estates were then sold to Peter Delmé of London whose ancestors had come to England from France in order to escape religious persecution. The Delmé family became the Lords of the Manor and initially took up residence at Place House, Titchfield, remaining there for the next 40 years after which they moved to Cams Hall in Fareham. In 1781 they abandoned Place House and deliberately demolished it with the exception of the gatehouse and an outer wall which can still be seen today.

By 1815, John Delmé of Cams Hall was the direct descendant holding the Titchfield Estates. In that year his exertion in drawing on his boot to go riding in the park caused a haemorrhage from which he died aged just 23. As he was childless the estates passed to his younger brother, Henry Peter Delmé, who was just on the point of going into action with his regiment in America. Henry returned to England, moved into Cams Hall, and held the Titchfield Estates right through until his death, aged 88, in 1883. As Henry also died childless the estates then passed in turn to his younger brother, Seymour Robert Delmé, who promptly sold his residence on the Isle of Wight and moved into Cams Hall. Seymour was the last of the original family of the Delmé name and when he died in 1894, aged 85 and childless, the estates, then comprising some 6,000 acres, passed to his nephews. By that time the Lee estate had already been sold off into other hands and vast changes were happening to it.

As recently as 1938 it was possible to walk from Stubbington, at the junction of Marks Road and Stubbington Lane, southwards to Manor Way in Lee along what was originally a medieval track (Milvil Lane). Half way along this lane between Lee and Stubbington there were still dwellings which were unoccupied. This hamlet was known as 'Millville' and the site would now be somewhere in the middle of the airfield. With its name 'Millville' and the fact that it was on the old medieval track, it does present itself as a contender for the location of the lost mill site.

At last we have arrived at the beginning …

2

THE LEE FAMILY ROBINSON

The extent to which Lee-on-the-Solent depended upon the Robinson family cannot be overstated. Indeed it is no exaggeration to say the town owes not only its name but also its very existence to them, their considerable energy and the large amounts of their personal fortune which they ploughed into the initial development of the resort.

For the purpose of this account we need to focus upon a father and two sons and, to appreciate what follows, it is necessary to have a brief insight into their lives through these three short biographical sketches.

Sir John Charles Robinson CB FSA (1824-1913)

John Charles Robinson was born in Nottingham on 16 December 1824 to Alfred Robinson. He was brought up in the town by his grandfather, a bookseller, and also received his education there. Initially he intended to become an architect but instead was sent to Paris for training as a painter, originally of landscapes and flowers. While there he spent much time in the Louvre developing his knowledge of Renaissance Art. Returning to England, he was appointed headmaster of the Government School of Art at Hanley in Staffordshire in 1847. He became a skilled etcher and was later a joint founder of the Royal Society of Painter Etchers.

On Christmas Eve 1852 he married Mary Anne (sometimes recorded as Marianne) Elizabeth Newton (1826-1908) at St Peter's Church, Stoke-on-Trent. She was the daughter of Edmund and Elizabeth Newton of Norwich and bore John five sons and two daughters:

Charles Edmund (later Charles Edmund Newton-Robinson) (b. 1853) barrister.

Emily (b. 1855).

Edmund Arthur (b. 1856) architect, surveyor and land agent.

Gerald Philip (b. 1858) artist and official mezzotint engraver to Her Majesty Queen Victoria.

Francis James (b. 1859) solicitor.

Frederick Sydney (b. 1863) for many years art master at Uppingham School, Rutland.

Marianne Isabella Napier (b. 1864).

Around the time of his marriage, he became the first superintendent of art collections at the South Kensington Museum (which later became the Victoria & Albert Museum) where he remained for the next 17 years. During this time he acquired a very extensive technical knowledge and appreciation of many branches of art and frequently travelled in Italy, France and Spain purchasing works for the Museum with the small funds at his disposal. Due to the turbulent times then prevailing in those countries, he was able to acquire for the Museum a vast number of valuable works in marble, bronze, majolica and terracotta at incredibly low prices, giving it a unique position among the museums of Europe. He resigned his post in 1869 as a result of a dispute but it is largely due to him that the V&A now houses one of the world's foremost collections of Renaissance art and sculpture.

Whilst employed by the Museum he also collected works of art for himself, as well as dealing in paintings on a private basis. Although such conduct was quite normal for those times, it would now be considered totally unacceptable for persons who, like him, were at the same time engaged in working for museums to behave and benefit in this way. Through this means, rather than by the sale of his own work, he acquired a considerable personal fortune.

On his retirement from public service, he became adviser to many prominent private art collectors and, from 1882 to 1901, he held the office of Crown Surveyor of Pictures to Her Majesty Queen Victoria. He was knighted in Jubilee year, 1887, and made a Companion of the Bath in 1901.

For many years he lived at 10 York Place in Marylebone and then at 107 Harley Street, London. In 1872 he purchased Newton Manor in Swanage, Dorset (now a Grade II listed building). The property had been empty for some years before and he carried out considerable works to the house and incorporated into it various architectural features which he had collected. His dining hall had a huge Tuscan fireplace, dating from about 1480, in black marble inside of which was a cast iron fireback with the royal coat of arms of Henry VIII from Hever Castle. The property became his home for the rest of his life.

He died as a result of a cerebral haemorrhage and heart failure at Newton Manor on 10 April 1913, aged 88. The house and contents were sold in August the same year; it then became a school, and in the 1970s was converted into multiple occupation. His eldest son, Charles, survived him by just eleven days.

Nineteenth century photograph of Sir John Charles Robinson — the founder of Lee-on-the-Solent

Charles Edmund Newton-Robinson MA (1853-1913)

Charles Edmund Robinson (he added his mother's maiden name of Newton to his surname in 1889 to distinguish himself from his father who was also often referred to as Charles Robinson) was the eldest child of John Charles Robinson and Mary Anne (or Marianne) Elizabeth Robinson. He was born at Kensington on 16 October 1853 and educated at Westminster School, where he was 'head of the water' for two seasons, and Trinity College Cambridge, where he excelled at running and hurdle jumping. He trained as a barrister at Inner Temple and was called to the Bar in 1879. In 1885 he married Jane Anna Stirk, daughter of Robert Stirk of Yorkshire but the couple did not have any children.

He collected works of art, both eagerly and incessantly, and created an important collection of Old Masters, engraved cameos and gems. In particular he made a special study of gemstones and became an expert in the field but he also had considerable further wide-ranging interests well beyond the art world. Much of his life was occupied with schemes of land development: the towns of Tankerton in Kent and Lee-on-the-Solent largely owe their existence to his efforts. The Land Taxes introduced by the Budget of 1909-1910 caused him to take an interest in politics. He founded and chaired The Land Union to resist interference with the interests of landowners and wrote a number of political articles.

He was a keen yachtsman and, in 1874, crossed the North Sea in a small sailing boat and explored the Dutch canals. He later wrote a book in 1876 entitled *The Cruise of the Widgeon* in which he described his journey. He part-designed, built and sailed many small racing yachts through 30 seasons of the Solent and South Coast Club Regattas. At these events he won many sailing accolades, indeed in one season alone his yacht *Corolla* secured 39 prizes out of 51 races in the Solent Matches.

Despite his yachting prowess, it was as a fencer that he was best known in England and on the Continent. He studied epée fencing in Paris in the 1890s and became an expert swordsman before returning home with a determination to revive swordsmanship in England. He persuaded a group of enthusiasts to establish the Epée Club of London in 1900 with the result that English fencers began to compete in Continental Tournaments for the first time. Thirteen competitors took part in the first open epée tournament on 5 May 1900 and Charles came second to the Frenchman Willy Sulzbacher, receiving a handsome silver medal for being the highest placed Englishman. In Paris, on 1 June of that same year, he became the first British fencer to take part in an Olympic Games, going out in the first round of the epée tournament. He was captain of the British epée team that fenced in the Coupe Internationale in Paris in 1904 and was a member of the British men's epée team which won a silver medal at the 1906 Intercalated Olympic Games in Athens. The article on the Epée de Combat in the 1911 edition of the *Encyclopaedia Britannica* was contributed by him.

In addition to writing *Picturesque Rambles in the Isle of Purbeck* in 1882, he also used his free time to write and publish poetry. His first volume was *The Golden Hind* in 1880. *Tintinnabula* followed in 1890 with *The Viol of Love* in 1895 and *Ver Lyrae* in 1896. Just before his death he completed *Moods and Metres* but did not live to see the initial proofs of it. His signature on the contract for its publication was the last word he ever wrote.

Towards the end of his life he suffered a long illness as a result of pancreatic cancer and became physically very weak. He died on 21 April 1913, aged 59, at Newton Manor, Swanage, Dorset.

Charles Edmund Newton-Robinson (standing left) with fellow members of the British Men's Epée Team at the 1906 Intercalated Olympic Games

One obituary to him read that he would be *remembered among his large circle of friends, not only for his most attractive personality, but also for his exceptionally wide range of knowledge and culture and for the many sidedness of his activities.*

Edmund Arthur Robinson (1856-1916)

Edmund Arthur Robinson was the third child and second son of John Charles Robinson and Mary Anne (or Marianne) Elizabeth Robinson. He was born at his parents' home at 25 Brompton Crescent, Brompton, London on 19 October 1856. He qualified as an architect and surveyor and, together with his father and older brother, played a prominent part in the development of Lee-on-the-Solent from an early stage including taking over the role of manager of the branch railway.

From the earliest days of such development, he took up permanent residence in the area and became the only member of the family to do so. At first he lived in Manor Way and then, in the 1890s, he moved to 'Melrose', a large villa on the corner of Milvil Road and Marine Parade West where he lived for the rest of his life. The site is now occupied by the West Point apartment block. He never married, and died, aged 59, at 'Melrose' on 14 April 1916 from the relatively rare condition of cancer of the soft palate.

3

LAND AHOY!

In the early 1880s, the area contained just a few small farms and cottages scattered over some tiny hamlets. There was some gravel extraction taking place although farming and fishing were the main occupations, the soil being fertile and the climate good, and the nearby waters provided a fine source of oysters and whiting. All of this was to change dramatically through the intervention of the Robinson family and their personal fortune.

How the area of Lee first came to the attention of the Robinsons is a matter of debate. The popular version of the story and the one which is generally quoted is that, through his extensive sailing interests already mentioned, Charles Edmund Robinson became very familiar with the waters of the Solent and the surrounding landscape; in 1883, while sailing his yacht in the Solent, his attention was drawn to the area of Lee. In particular he felt that the natural beach and cliffs would provide a marvellous location for the development of a seaside resort that, in time, might rival the likes of Bournemouth or Southsea. Charles discussed his ideas for such a development with his father, who agreed to provide the finance necessary to run the programme from his personal fortune. There is no contemporary evidence supporting this story, but there is another possibility which the authors favour as being the more likely sequence of events.

As mentioned earlier, John Robinson was appointed Crown Surveyor of Pictures to Her Majesty Queen Victoria in 1882 when he was aged 60. In this capacity he would have been required to visit Osborne House on the Isle of Wight on a number of occasions. In the speech which he delivered at the opening ceremony of the railway in 1894, he said of Lee-on-the-Solent that he *could scarcely realise that it had become a town which was the first sight on which the eyes of the Queen rested in her island home.* This strongly suggests that, on what was probably his first visit to Osborne House, *his* eyes rested on the shoreline across the Solent. He had already demonstrated his strong business acumen in amassing his personal fortune and had, by this time, already ventured into land development in Swanage in his own right (see Appendix 5) without any particular involvement of his sons. Bearing in mind the patriarchal nature of society in Victorian times, this does raise the question whether John Robinson suggested to, or even instructed, his son Charles, when he was next sailing in the Solent, to check that part of coastline and report back to him. He would then look at the possibility of developing an estate in that area. There was a wooden jetty at the site of the future pier and so it would have been quite possible to get ashore and view the land. In one of the earliest plans of the estate of J C Robinson it is quite clear that the focus of the estate is centred on Victoria Square. This further suggests a link to Osborne House. Final support for this theory is given in a now almost forgotten paragraph tucked away in the Society Gossip column of *The Hampshire Advertiser* of Saturday 6 September 1884 which states that John Robinson's *attention had been directed to the advantages of the site during one of his official visits to Osborne.* In the end it does not really matter which version is correct as the result was the same – the Robinsons had arrived and John and his sons, Charles and Edmund, would be the key players in the new venture.

Contracts for the purchase of the land were drawn up and completed by the agents for the local landowner and John Charles Robinson in 1883. This covered about 220 acres with a second purchase of about 32 acres being made later that year. Working from the Titchfield Tithe Map it can be calculated that, by the end of the year, the Robinson family had acquired a little over 264 acres and owned a sea frontage of almost 7,000ft *[2,130m]*. At that time the rate assessment records show that, in the whole estate purchased, there was a total of just seven assessments yielding an aggregate value of £279 4s 6d *[£22,500]*.

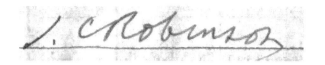

Sir John Charles Robinson's personal signature which set the seal on the development of Lee

The idea of the new name of Lee-on-the-Solent is reputed to have come from one of the family's agents, W Herbert Hannen. The family set up the Lee-on-the-Solent Estates Company to undertake the building operations and sales marketing and, from this point, the initial development of the resort under the influence of the family can be conveniently divided into three main phases – land plots, pier and railway.

4

STARTING FROM SCRATCH

The first phase of development commenced almost immediately and comprised the construction of the first few roads around the seafront, the laying of sewers and drainage and the division of the land into plots to be offered for sale. Individual buyers would be responsible for developing their own plots. Each plot was sold in the name of John Charles Robinson and, in order to try to establish the character which the family sought for the area, he imposed restrictive covenants on many plots prohibiting the establishment of anything other than a single private dwelling house. Such covenants remain on many of the legal titles to this day but, as there is now no one with a legal right to enforce them, blocks of flats have sprung up with impunity on many of the old plots, especially along the seafront and in the High Street.

The roads which are now called Manor Way and Pier Street already existed as tracks and provided the only route down to the sea when the Robinson family bought the estate in 1883. These were upgraded in the first stages of development of the town. Running out from them, the other first few roads developed on the new estate were Newton Place, a small section of Grove Road on the eastern side of Manor Way, Marine Parade East (but stopping short of the present junction with Portsmouth Road) and a short section of Cambridge Road (running up from Marine Parade and turning right for short stretch before stopping at the present junction with Gosport Road).

Marine Parade was the brainchild of the Robinson family. When completed it was over a mile in length and laid out to run parallel with the cliff. It was 50 feet wide *[15.25m]* and had a grass belt reserved as a park, 150 feet *[45.75m]* in width, between it and the cliff edge.

Only the north side was to be developed so that the open vista to the Solent and the Isle of Wight beyond would be maintained and, in the ensuing years, a line of red brick villas would flank the road. One of the first buildings to appear along here was 'Trafalgar House' (see Chapter 9). In Pier Street, which was originally called Pier Road, some early commercial premises were constructed in the 1890s but on the eastern side only, the western side being left undeveloped and lined with trees right up to the mid 1930s.

Early commercial development in Pier Street

Marketing of the land in the new development was carried out by the family and the Estates Company very enthusiastically. Brochures were produced showing the plots which were available for sale and a long series of auctions, usually conducted by Mr F G Wheatley or Mr E H Lumley, were held regularly. The auctions were often held at the Assembly Room which was adjacent to the Victoria Hotel (later renamed The Bun Penny, which relates to the way the Queen is wearing her hair on the coins) in Manor Way. The very first auction commenced at 3pm on 3 September 1884 and comprised 47 lots, all of which were situated along Manor Way and in Marine Parade East. In the notice published for that auction the sellers were keen to point out that: *The building conditions will be almost unrestricted, and the terms of payment only require 10 per cent of* the purchase money to be paid down, the balance payable by instalments in nine years. Later, when a railway link was established, special trains were laid on to bring in prospective buyers.

An indication of the way in which these sales were conducted and the prices realised can be gleaned from an article appearing in *The Portsmouth Evening News* of Thursday 29 August 1889:

The twentieth sale of freehold building sites was held yesterday at the Victoria Hotel when 50 lots were submitted by Mr. H. Lumley, and every lot sold straight off the reel. The pier band discoursed lively music, and a hearty welcome to all visitors was accorded by Mr. Charles and Mr. Edmund Robinson, Mr. Lumley and Mr. and Mrs. Hannen, at the old "Victoria". After an enjoyable walk around the estate, luncheon was served with champagne, ad libitum. At the sale there were nearly one hundred persons, including several ladies. Prefacing the sale, some practical remarks were made by Mr. Charles Robinson (who presided at the luncheon), respecting the development of the estate. He said the day had gone by for any opposition to be lodged against the new railway, which would be in a forward state, if not completed, a year hence. Some gentlemen had formed a syndicate to erect a new hotel near the Pier, [the pier was opened in 1888 – see Chapter 5] *and a pavilion had been erected on the Pier, and the band would continue to play till the end of the season. The whole of the houses built on the estate were occupied, and further accommodation was applied for every day. There were already over 200 freeholders. The sale commenced with*

Three lots in Marine Parade, one frontage of 106ft *[32.25m]*, and two frontages of 40ft *[12.25m]*. They fetched respectively £157 10s *[£14,000]*, £120 *[£10,650]* and £137 10s *[£12,200]*;

Eight lots in Montserrat Road of 40ft *[12.25m]* frontage, bought from £58 10s *[£5,200]* to £62 10s *[£5,500]*;

Three lots in Victoria Square of 40ft *[12.25m]* frontage, £57 10s *[£5,100]*, £75 *[£6,650]*, £65 *[£5,750]*;

Four lots in Milvil Road and Victoria Square, one 50ft *[15.25m]* frontage, £87 10s *[£7,750]*, three 58ft *[17.75m]* frontages, £90 *[£8,000]* each;

Four more lots in Victoria Square, one of 50ft *[15.25m]* frontage, £85 *[£7,550]*; and – Three 40ft *[12.25m]* frontages, £62 10s *[£5,500]*, £63 *[£5,600]*, and £54 *[£4,800]*;

Twelve lots in Raynes Road of 30ft *[9.25m]*, from £29 *[£2,550]* to £33 *[£2,950]*;

Four lots in South Place of 27½ft *[8.5m]*, £26 *[£2,300]* a plot;

Three lots in Ryde Place, of 27½ ft *[8.5m]*, £25 *[£2,200]*, £25 10s *[£2,250]* and £26 10s *[£2,350]*;

Two shop plots in Portsmouth Road, of 25ft *[7.5m]* frontage, £32 *[£2,850]* each.

The amount realised at the sale was £2,640 10s [£235,000].

Obviously Sir John Robinson was aware that his vision of a residential seaside resort with large villas for the wealthy Victorians would require a local workforce to meet the needs of the new residents. Although he carried out many charitable acts, it seems likely that the building of the humbler properties for the workforce in the orderly grid pattern of roads in Elmore was more a question of necessity than a philanthropic gesture. Elmore was far enough away so that the occupants would not intrude upon privacy of the residents of villas and mansions. The pumping station for the sewerage system was located near the present sailing club boatyard at Elmore and the discharge pipe had its outlet about half a mile out to sea.

Geological maps show the presence of Brickearth in an area in the northern part of Cherque. As the name suggests, it is used in the making of bricks, and the brick-making industry was very important in the Gosport area from Tudor times up to the first decade of the twentieth century. At one of the auctions held in September 1886, Charles Robinson announced that it was: *important for intending purchasers of land to know that they had started brick burning on the estate, which meant a considerable reduction in the price of the principal material used in the construction of buildings. They were now able to supply bricks at 25s [£109] per thousand, which was about as low as it was possible to get them. There was an abundance of sand and gravel on the estate, indeed, everything necessary for building was in easy reach*. Interestingly one of the earliest rows of houses built in Elmore, which was originally closest to Cherque, was Brickland Terrace in Gosport Road.

As the estate developed it was necessary to provide and maintain basic services and the sewerage system has been mentioned briefly. The Lee-on-the-Solent Waterworks Company was formed in 1891 to erect the water works and the site chosen for this was just north of the junction of Grove Road and Studland Road. Another facility was established on the south-east side of Beach Road, adjacent to the railway line, where there were naturally occurring springs. A water tower for the supply of water to parts of the town was located at the western end of the present Salisbury Terrace with the junction of Cambridge Road and a large storage tank was positioned on the southern edge of Elmore Lake. In 1904 an Act was passed to enable the Gosport Waterworks Company to take over the undertakings of the local company.

At the same time that the Waterworks Company was commencing its operations, the Gosport Gas and Coke Company made arrangements to extend its mains supply to the area. The plans prepared by the Company still exist and show that the supply was initially limited only to routes along Manor Way and Grove Road; the upper end of Milvil Road, Norwich Place and Nottingham Place; Marine Parade West to Pier Street, High Street and Beach Road; Marine Parade East to Beach Road; Portsmouth Road; the eastern half of Cambridge Road; Gosport Road eastwards to Cross Road only; Elmore Road. No other roads were included in the supply shown.

In December 1927, Portsmouth Corporation decided to extend the electricity mains supply to Lee-on-the-Solent. Once again the correspondence and plans from this time still exist and show it was concluded that the most convenient route was from Titchfield. The supply ran from Titchfield High Street via Bridge Street and Hollam Farm then south along the road to Crofton and thence into Lee.

5

PIERING OUT TO SEA

With the sale of the plots of development land proceeding apace, the second main phase of the development was ready to be undertaken. The idea of constructing a pier was part of the family's initial plans for the development of the seaside resort when the land was purchased in 1883. The intention was to replace, in the same position, a small wooden jetty which had been in use up to that time.

The site for the building of the pier had been conveyed to John Robinson at a nominal annual rent of one shilling *[£4.30] if demanded*. In 1885 an Act of Parliament authorised the construction of the pier and, in July of that year, John Robinson's wife, Marianne, unveiled the foundation stone. The design chosen for the pier was that submitted by Messrs Galbraith and Church and the appointed contractor was Mr F Bevis of St Thomas's Street, Portsmouth. John Robinson personally financed the £8,500 *[£737,500]* needed to carry out the construction. The main work commenced in 1886 and by autumn of the following year the pier was complete with the exception of the entrance building. This was constructed shortly after by Mr Wareham of Titchfield at a cost of £334 *[£29,250]* to the design of Mr Horace A Alexander, architect, of 72 Cannon Street, London. That building would later be demolished in 1934 to make way for the construction of the Tower complex.

The Robinson family formed the Lee-on-the-Solent Pier Company with a share capital of £12,500 *[£1,092,000]* in £5 *[£440]* shares with the intention that the Company would then buy the pier from John Robinson and run it thereafter. The Company directors were John Robinson and his son Charles, Horace Alexander, Alfred

Ernest Petrie and Thomas Andrew Raynes (these last two had roads in Lee-on-the-Solent named after them). Unfortunately, although the pier was an immediate success with the public, there was no great enthusiasm for the purchase of shares in the Company, with the result that the pier remained in the personal ownership of John Robinson for many years beyond that envisaged by the family. In fact by 1904 all of the shares were held by the Robinson family and it was only due to their action in that year that the Company was finally able to take over legal ownership.

The pier structure started from a sea wall of Portland cement and concrete blocks and was 750 feet *[230m]* long. For the first 600 feet *[185m]* it was 15 feet *[4.5m]* wide but then expanded to 34 feet *[10.25m]* wide for the remainder of the 150 feet *[45m]* pier-head. This area, known as 'the Golden Hall', housed a small pavilion and bandstand. A contemporary report of the time stated that *cast iron screw piles, driven in about an average of 9 feet [2.75m] into the sea bed, support the superstructure, which consists of wrought iron piles, strongly braced together with angle-iron bars, and united longitudinally by wrought iron lattice girders, which carry the joists of the deck. The whole is surmounted by a neat iron railing. At the seaward extremity are timber fender piles, and along the eastern side of the pier-head extends a landing stage for steamers and boats, composed of massive timber piling, well braced, and abutting against iron screw piles driven diagonally, to take the thrust of vessels coming alongside, and relieve the main structure from strains arising.* The pier was also provided with seats and glazed shelters.

On 3 April 1888 a ceremony was held at which Lady Robinson returned to formally open the pier. Of that occasion *The Hampshire Telegraph* dated 7 April 1888 reported:

The band of the 3rd Volunteer Battalion Hampshire Regiment from Gosport, was in attendance, and played lively selections. The ceremony, which was performed by Lady Robinson, was brief. Her Ladyship at a given signal severed the satin ribbon which had been suspended across the Pier-head, and declared the structure open. Cheers followed for her Ladyship and Sir Charles Robinson, the promoter of the new watering place. Afterwards a luncheon was provided at the Victoria Hotel, Lee-on-the-Solent. Sir Charles Robinson presided... The day's proceedings concluded with sports on the beach.

Looking landward from the pier, 1893

Yachts, steamers and small boats landed passengers at all times of the tide with *Princess Beatrice* being the first steamer to call on the opening day. Originally it had been planned to have a steamer link between Lee-on-the-Solent, the Isle of Wight, Southampton, Portsmouth and Southsea, but it was only viable to operate a service in the summer months to Southsea. The steam launch *Venus*, owned by the New Steam Launch Company of Portsmouth, made eight trips per day between Lee-on-the-Solent and Clarence Pier at Southsea at a return fare of one shilling *[£4.50]* and a trip time of 45 minutes. This operated from May until the end of September and was a popular run. In the 1893 season for example, she carried some 22,000 passengers. Whilst the main steamer companies in the area did not make scheduled stops at the pier, in March 1923 a service was introduced by Lloyd's Motor Packet Service running between Southampton, Lee-on-the Solent and Cowes. This also proved to be very popular.

In *An Historical Guide to the Pleasure Resorts & Places of Interest in the County (Hampshire and Isle of Wight) 1893*, concerning Lee-on-the-Solent the author writes: *From the beach, close by the pier, open* sailing boats with safe breadth of beam can be hired, together with skiffs and rowing boats, on most moderate terms. Whiting and other fish are caught in goodly numbers, about a mile off the shore, and anglers from the pier head will not go unrewarded. There are bathing machines and tents upon the beach, which is of great length, and composed of sand and fine shingle. The tide has a rise and fall of 12 feet [3.75m] or more, and the sea-bottom being composed of a level bed of sand, bathing is perfectly safe whatever the state of the tide, and little ones can paddle to their heart's content. There are no sudden deceptive shelving banks of sand, which cause bathers to find themselves abruptly launched into water, in which they immediately realise that they are out of their depth.

Crowds enjoying a sunny day on the beach near the pier, c.1906

Tragedies still happened, however. In July 1920 a sad incident occurred when the body of Grace Trench, a young Gosport woman, was found in the sea about 600ft [180m] from the pier. To her body was tied a cord to which were attached two shoemaker's iron lasts. Two handkerchiefs were lightly knotted around her ankles. A pathetic farewell letter to her boyfriend was found at the pier, the pencilled message emphasising that she had committed suicide and had not been murdered. She also left a note to her father, pencilled as she sat on the pier in the dark waiting for the tide to come in, requesting that she be buried at sea.

Another tragedy happened some three years later when, in August 1923, Wilfred Cyril Lipscombe, a five-year-old from Shedfield who was on an outing to Lee, reached for a balloon from the steps of the pier, fell into the water and was drowned.

In the mid 1920s, The Official Town Guide to Lee-on-the-Solent was able to announce that concerts, whist drives and teas were a daily feature of the activities on the pier and that rowing boats were available for hire "at reasonable terms".

There was always a small admission charge levied for access onto the pier. In the 1930s the tariff for each child was 1d. *[22p]* although a special concession of free entry was given to any child who was a member of *The Daily Mail*'s 'Teddy Tail Club' and was sporting the appropriate badge to show this. Of course children easily found ways to circumvent having to pay. It was not unusual for the only badge holder in a group of children to go on to the pier. Having gained free admission he would then drop the badge over to the others who stood underneath waiting to catch it so that the next one could walk on ... and so on until the whole group had managed to get on for nothing!

Sadly, in 1932, disaster struck when an electrical fault, believed to have been in a connection between a navigation light and the pavilion radio, caused a fire which destroyed the pavilion. One report of the time stated that *the Pavilion was transformed during a tragic half-hour from a fairy-like structure that shimmered silver in the summer haze to a blackened mass of twisted steel girders and wooden piles — a complete wreck.*

The fire broke out during the afternoon lull on Sunday 19 June. An hour earlier the lunch rush had been at its height and an hour later the beautiful maple floor of the Pavilion would have been crowded with several hundred people attending the tea dance. As it was, 50 people had to grope their way to safety through dense choking smoke and three anglers at the end of the pier had to leap into the sea for safety. The Gosport Fire Brigade was called out but, by the time they arrived, it was clear that they would be unable to save the structure, so they demolished part of the decking to act as a firebreak and to prevent the flames from spreading further along the pier. The crew remained on the scene until the very late hours to ensure that the flames had all been extinguished and that there was no risk of any further outbreak. There were no injuries but the resident musicians, the Harry Lawrence Dance Band, lost instruments worth £500 *[£27,100]* and the total damage to the structure was estimated at £35,000 *[£1,890,000]*. Regrettably no work was ever undertaken to make good the damage and was it was left in its sorry state. No longer the attraction it had been, the remains of the pier were largely used as a promenade and for fishing.

The disastrous pier fire of 19 June 1932

By 1938 the pier was in receivership and negotiations with Gosport Council were taking place for the local authority to acquire the structure, but the advent of war caused all progress to come to a halt.

In July 1940, wartime measures were invoked to close the area around the pier and sections of the ironwork were blown up to prevent it from being used in the event of a German invasion. Although this was a rather futile act, it was another nail in the coffin. The decline was then exacerbated when heavy seas proceeded to wash away some of the landward end of the structure.

As part of the preparations for D-Day in 1944, it was decided that Lee-on-the-Solent would be the headquarters for CO-TUG, the Anglo-American tug unit responsible for organising the transport of Mulberry Harbour components to Normandy. The main Operation Overlord tug-assembly area was in the waters off Lee-on-the-Solent and a stores depot was located on the pier. When the forces were assembled on the cliffs at Lee-on-the-Solent immediately prior to D-Day, the US Army effected a temporary repair to the pier. A ramp was built from the promenade about 55 yards *[50m]* to the east of the pier to the platform at the end. It took only a day to construct but was an important means of embarkation for some of the forces going over to Normandy.

After the War, Gosport Council did acquire ownership and announced plans to renovate the pier using funds received from the War Damage Commission, but those funds were spent elsewhere on other projects and it became clear that no restoration work would be undertaken.

In the summer of 1956, Robin Martin and Ian Harris were scuba-diving around the skeletal remains of the end of the pier searching for lobsters. This was quite a lucrative activity and generally they sold their catch to one of the bank managers in Lee-on-the-Solent. During one dive they came across some blocks. At first they assumed these to be simple slabs of concrete but, with some difficulty, they managed to get one to the surface and proceeded to break it up by throwing it down on the landing jetty part of the pier. They then discovered that the slabs were in fact brass trays filled with concrete.

Salvage discovery day, 1956

There were a number of these trays, each of which measured about 4ft *[1.25m]* by 15 inches *[40cm]* and were about 4 inches *[10cm]* deep. Fixed to the top of each tray was a brass plate about half an inch *[1cm]* thick. The tray they recovered was taken by rowing boat to the beach at Elmore; Robin and Ian teamed up with Paul Urry and the item was stored at Paul's home. For most of the summer weekends the three divers, with the assistance of a few helpers, set about salvaging the remaining brass trays. A block and tackle was tied to one of the horizontal girders to pull up the trays which were again transported to the beach at Elmore where the concrete was removed. Many of the plates were no longer connected to the trays, but all the items were taken to Paul's home and stored until everything had been retrieved. In all about two tons of brass was collected and, when it was taken to the Receiver of Wrecks and Salvage Depot in Southampton, the divers were informed that the trays were probably the remains of the cladding of a gun emplacement installed at the end of the pier by the Americans.

Two years after this, in 1958, the remnants of the pier were finally demolished thus bringing to an end one of the very early and most popular attractions of the town.

6

MAKING TRACKS TO
WHERE THE RAINBOW
ENDS

With the pier complete, the Robinson family turned their attention to the third stage of development. They felt that transport access to the resort needed to be improved by connecting it with the nearby national railway network and, to this end, the Lee-on-the-Solent Railway Company was incorporated on 5 July 1890 with a share capital of £30,000 *[£2,660,000]* in £10 *[£885]* shares. The original promoters of the company were William Stephen Cross, James Edward Hunter, Charles Edward Morgan, Harry Emans Pollard (who was Chairman of the Board of Directors) and Charles Langley Whetham. Mr G A Petter was appointed as company secretary.

Initially the plan had been to run a railway line direct from Fareham to Lee-on-the-Solent and a provisional application for powers to enable this to proceed was submitted on 15 November 1888. It soon became clear, however, that a more reasonable option, from a financial point of view, was the building of a light railway line a little over three miles long and branching off from the main line at Fort Brockhurst. This would provide a connection to London via Southampton.

Mr R H Tigg was appointed to carry out a survey of the line and to provide an estimate of the likely costs, which he placed at £18,684 *[£1,655,000]* with a contingency fund of £1,868 8s 0d *[£16,550]*. On 14 April 1890 Parliament unanimously granted powers under the Railway Construction Facilities Act of 1864 to enable to venture to proceed. In fact this railway was one of the very few to be built under this particular piece of legislation. In November 1890 the contract for the construction of the line was awarded to Messrs David Laing &

Sons of London at a value of £24,375 *[£2,160,000]* and Mr F Gillham was appointed consulting engineer to oversee the works.

A foundation ceremony took place on 22 October 1890 to start work at the site of the terminus which, it was decided, should be located next to the newly completed pier. Sir John Robinson and his son, Charles, were in attendance and *The Hampshire Telegraph* of Saturday 25 October 1890 reported:

Mr Pollard cut the first turf, amidst enthusiastic cheering, and a plough proceeded to cut up the line of turf to show the route of the railway ... At the invitation of Sir Charles Robinson those present at the ceremony were entertained at a champagne luncheon in the Assembly Rooms, at the Victoria Hotel at which Mr. N. Robinson presided.

Progress on the building of the railway was extremely slow. Whether it was a question of finance or the style of train carriages (which determined the height of the platforms) that caused the delay, almost no work had been done on the line by April of the following year. The construction engineer resigned in November 1891 and a whole year later Sir John Robinson had to come to the rescue by using his own funds to buy all the remaining unsold shares in the company. This cash injection provided the impetus which was so badly needed. Early in 1893 new contractors, Messrs Pauling & Elliot of Westminster, were appointed to build the line; Mr Patrick W Meik became the new consulting engineer in February 1893 and Mr I B Ivatts took on the job of line manager. Around this time about 100 men were employed building the line, good progress was made and few difficulties were encountered in construction, as the only major ground-work was the construction of a bridge over the River Alver.

By 24 March 1893 all the works had been completed and the required report on the line was submitted to the Board of Trade as a prerequisite for the official inspection of the railway. It is clear from the report that, in order to save costs on the employment of crossing keepers, all the level crossings along the line were to be operated by the train crews themselves. There were, in fact, four such crossings at Elmore, Browndown, Privett and Pound Lane. On 15 July 1893 Major Yorke carried out the official inspection of the line and promptly failed it on no less than 13 points, largely because he felt that some of the required work was still incomplete.

By early the following year, the company had ensured that all of the outstanding issues had been addressed and, at the re-inspection by the Board of Trade on 7 May 1894, the line was passed as fit for use. With the line thus finally complete, the railway was able to open for passenger service on Saturday 12 May 1894. This was just in time for the Whit Monday holiday on which over 1,000 visitors arrived at the resort on the railway excursions laid on for that occasion. Yet even these were not enough to deal with the demand and many potential visitors never made it to their destination but were left behind, because the trains to Lee-on-the-Solent were full.

Establishing the railway track (top right), 1893

On Thursday 31 May 1894, the ceremony to mark the formal opening of the line was performed by the Countess of Clanwilliam at Lee-on-the-Solent railway station. A special train was laid on from Waterloo to Fort Brockhurst Station to bring down the VIP guests. The group then transferred to the branch line for the onward journey to Lee-on-the-Solent. Other guests arrived by steam launch from Southsea. The entire party was met at the terminus by Charles Robinson where the area was festooned with flags and bunting. Sir John and Lady Robinson were in attendance once again as was the line manager, Mr Ivatts. After a short service and ceremony, at which the Countess was presented with a key to the station, the whole party proceeded to the Assembly Room at the Victoria Hotel where luncheon was served by the proprietor, Mr Hannen, and speeches were made. *The Portsmouth Evening News* of Friday 1 June 1894 reported:

After lunch the toast list was commenced with the "Health of the Queen", proposed by Sir John Charles Robinson. Mr. W.S.J. Wilde next proposed the health and happiness of Sir John Charles Robinson and Lady Robinson, without whom, he said, the event for which they were gathered would never have come to pass. There was no question that Lee-on-the-Solent was a very healthful, airy, place. The railway appeared to be very well laid, and everything ran very smoothly. Sir John Charles Robinson thanked them for the honour. He remarked that it was difficult for him to realise the full import of the matter which had brought them together. When he first remembered that ten years ago the place was nothing but a lone, outlying farm by the sea-side, tenanted only by sheep, cows and pigs and a few rustics devoted in bringing up the animals, he could scarcely realise that it had become a town which was the first sight on which the eyes of the Queen rested in her island home. His sons had taken the chief part in the undertaking, and to them was undoubtedly due most of the success. It had been a very arduous undertaking, endless difficulties had had to be grappled with and overcome — so great indeed, that he had been more than once tempted to ask himself whether it was not a crime to build a new railway in England. However as they saw, they had managed to pull through at last.

The remains of the Fort Brockhurst Station building can still be seen alongside the road at the traffic lights at the junction of Military Road and Station Road, near Brune Park School. The line then ran roughly parallel to, and on the east side of, Military Road (the route of an ancient road) along to where the Cocked Hat public house now stands. As late as the 1950s buffers could still be seen there. The

Lee-on-the-Solent Railway terminus

route then curved westward and there was a level crossing with a Halt approximately where there is now a car sales centre at Gomer roundabout. This Halt was named Privett Halt although the name was later changed to Fort Gomer Halt. For many years there was no shelter on this platform until one was erected in February 1920 at a cost of £245 *[£7,680]*.

The track then followed the path of the current road on the north side of Browndown Camp to Lee-on-the-Solent, up to where the present traffic lights are on the junction of Privett Road and Cherque Way. Before the current road was built this was barren land, marshy in places, and known locally as the Warren. At the location of these traffic lights there was another level crossing and just on the other side of the existing wire fence was the location of Browndown Halt. This was just an open platform which never did have any shelter for passengers.

The railway track then ran parallel to, and on the south side of, Portsmouth Road, curving round at Elmore at the junction of Queens Road and Marine Parade East, where eventually Elmore Halt was situated. During the Second World War, although the train service had long since been defunct, there were still the remains of the concrete platform of Elmore Halt at the site of the current sailing club boatyard.

The line then followed the coast along the top of the cliffs to the Lee-on-the-Solent Station terminus near the present skateboard park. The station building, which once accommodated a general as well as a ladies' waiting room, an office/booking hall, a porter's room, store and lavatories is now an amusement arcade. Immediately next door to the railway station, in the building which is now an Asian restaurant, was a tea-room. Next door to that, on the corner with Marine Parade East, and on the end of what later became known as Flower Buildings, was the office of the Lee-on-the-Solent Railway Company.

An early view of Lee-on-the-Solent Railway Station with tea-room next door to its left. The wooden hut in the foreground is the original premises of the local Sailing Club (see Chapter 25). Background left is Pier Hotel (see Chapter 11) and background right is Heylands Court Hotel (see Chapter 11)

One interesting feature shown on early plans of the line is the marking of an additional proposed curve and points near Fort Brockhurst Station to take the line south and directly onto the main track towards Gosport. The land for this appears to have been owned by the company and the construction of the curve would have allowed trains to run directly from Gosport to Lee and back without the need for passengers to enter into, or change at, Fort Brockhurst Station.

Clearly this would have made access much easier and at relatively modest additional cost, but the plan never came to fruition and we are left to speculate upon how the fate of the line might have been different had the curve and points been installed.

Another point of interest is that, although the company had sufficient land to enable the whole length of the line to be a double track, only a single track was ever constructed. No doubt it was felt that doubling the line would be an unnecessary expense, especially as it had been resolved from the outset to only ever have one train running along the route at any one time. This in turn meant that there was never any need for signalling along any part of the line – another matter which must have saved on the cost of construction.

When the line opened, the service comprised six trains each way daily, with five on Sundays, between Lee-on-the-Solent and Fort Brockhurst, with all services calling by request at the two intermediate Halts at Browndown and Privett. The total journey time was 20 minutes which may appear to be rather slow, and indeed it was, as the Board of Trade stipulated a maximum speed limit of just 10mph! Following yet another official inspection on 5 November 1894 the Board appears to have consented to the speed limit being increased to 15mph which then cut the journey time to 15 minutes. As the journey time from Waterloo to Fort Brockhurst Station was just under 2 hours 45 minutes, with one change at Fort Brockhurst it was possible to travel from Waterloo to Lee-on-the-Solent in just over three hours. The single journey fare between termini was 3d [£1.15] for third class, 6d [£2.30], for second class and 9d [£3.45] for first class. A report appearing in *The Hampshire Telegraph* edition of Saturday 19 May 1894 gave a somewhat lyrical insight into the journey along the line from Lee-on-the-Solent to Fort Brockhurst:

… and the train is going. "All aboard", and off she glides amid friendly farewells, past the busily working windmill that draws from a well within a few yards of the shore the supplies of fresh water that are necessary for the engine; on to Browndown, where the tented field presents to the eye a microcosm of that "armed camp of Europe" about which after dinner orators are so fond of

talking when they respond for "The Army". A youth stands on the Browndown platform, calmly holding a red flag, at the sight of which the train comes to a halt, and allows a red-coated marksman, who had been class-firing at the butts to step on. Then off again, until Privett is reached where another red flag is waved, and another stop is made to take up a lady. A few more leisurely puffs, and we are at Fort Brockhurst Station, close to the tram which is to carry us away from the pleasant association of Lee-on-the-Solent and its railway line into the busy world of Gosport.

Initially, in addition to Fort Brockhurst Station on the main line, only Lee-on-the-Solent Station was manned. Here there was a stationmaster and two staff and at one time a bookstall run by W H Smith was established within the station building. The intermediate halts remained unmanned throughout although later a stationmaster, Mr Fairweather, was appointed to look after Browndown Halt. It was felt that this was necessary, especially as he could supervise the point where the line crossed Portsmouth Road.

Unfortunately the railway was never destined to be the success that the Robinson family, the operating company and those around them might have wished and it failed to attract the customers and make the profits the company had anticipated. In the first month the receipts were a mere £30 3s 5d [£2,750] whereas the outgoings for wages alone for the same period were £39 10s 6d [£3,600]. This was to be the normal trend within the accounts and often there was barely enough in the coffers to pay the staff wages. Additionally, goods traffic was particularly poor and yielded little income and the operators were soon in debt. By the end of the first year the railway had already incurred an operating deficit of £84 8s 11d [£7,850]. Shortly after the line opened the manager, Mr Ivatts, resigned and his role was taken over by Edmund Arthur Robinson.

Passenger numbers at Browndown Halt were quite reasonable as it was used by service personnel travelling to and from the firing ranges, and in the summer it provided a useful stopping place for people wishing to have a Sunday walk or picnic in the country. Nevertheless, the overall numbers of passengers using the branch line was far from being economically viable. It rather appears that, when the railway company had been set up, not enough thought had been given to who would use the branch line. The people travelling to and from London would only provide a limited customer base. Other local inhabitants were unlikely to benefit greatly in being transported to Fort Brockhurst and then transferring to a tram to get to the centre of Gosport or to the ferry. It did not provide a reasonable alternative to taking a bus from Lee-on-the-Solent direct into Gosport, despite the rather tortuous route followed by the road. Consequently the railway company had an almost impossible task in competing with motor-buses on convenience.

One also wonders if the company's heart was in the project. In Sir Charles Robinson's speech at the opening of the railway he said that he had been more than once tempted to ask himself whether it was not a crime to build a new railway in England. As early as 1896, a mere two years after the opening of the branch line, discussions were being conducted concerning the possible take-over by the London & South Western Railway (LSWR). However the line remained independent and was still losing money. In 1908 the annual expenditure was £1,102 [£89,700] but receipts for the year were only £700 [£57,000]. Whilst the number of trains by this time had increased to eight daily each way, the Sunday service had been reduced to a mere three each way. A large part of the attraction of the line must have been due to the fact that it ran to the seaside. Therefore one can only speculate on how much this reduction in services, on what must have been a prime day for casual visitors, would have affected the potential receipts. The situation was made even worse when, by the time of the Great War, all Sunday services were withdrawn completely and never reinstated.

On 26 July 1909 LSWR assumed the power to operate the line. It changed the name of the Halt at Privett to Fort Gomer because there was another Privett near East Meon, and opened a new Halt at Elmore on 11 April 1910 to cater for the growth in housing at that end of the town. To alight at this Halt it was necessary to give advance notice to the guard on board the train. Passengers wishing to board the train at Elmore Halt were required to follow the instructions set out on a notice displayed in the shelter on the platform. This stated that they were first required to attend at the bakery premises on the opposite side of Portsmouth Road where they were to request the baker to release his boy when the train was due, so that he could run down the line towards the approaching train waving a red flag!

Despite the new arrangements with LSWR, the ownership of the line together with all of the accumulated debts remained with the Lee-on-the-Solent Railway Company. LSWR had already notified the company that the two hired locomotives it was using had exceeded their useful life and needed to be replaced. As there were no suitable locomotives available, LSWR ran the service with rail motors.

Notwithstanding the opening the Halt at Elmore, the company continued to lose money. In 1910 guards were withdrawn from the branch line and this resulted in difficulties in collecting fares from passengers travelling between Halts and a further fall in revenue.

During the Great War the State took control of the railways, which is possibly why, in 1915, LSWR reverted to the use of locomotive haulage on this branch line.

A description of the line from around 1919 was provided in G A Allcock's book, *Gosport's Railway Era*:

The train would travel alongside the Military Road as far as Gomer Halt — the area was often flooded and the railway engineers had great difficulty in crossing the bed of the River Alver. Browndown Halt was situated at the beginning of Portsmouth Road. It was just a bare platform but actually had a Station Master who was in charge of the crossing gates. The track proceeded along Portsmouth Road which was a gravel lane. Elmore Halt had a cutting and a board marked "Whistle", a level crossing and a wicket gate, a small platform and a shelter and a name board. Across the road was a baker's shop where one could buy a delicious iced bun to munch whilst sitting on the fence waiting for the train. From Elmore Halt the line to Lee-on-Solent was a straight run.

On arrival at Lee Station the train crew would shunt the engine back to the water tower to refill the water tanks and then they would disappear to the

Working Men's Club, which was a former chapel, to refuel themselves before making the return journey back to Fort Brockhurst.

The Lee-on-the-Solent railway was advertised as taking passengers "to where the rainbow ends". This phrase was echoed in a notice displayed later in a different context in an estate agent's office (see Chapter 16).

In 1921, the railways were still state controlled and David Lloyd George's government passed the Railway Act, also known as the Grouping Act, which eventually led to the nationalisation of the railways in 1947. The purpose of the Act was to try to stem the losses being suffered by many of the 120 railway companies. The working of the rail system was reorganised by consolidating companies into four main groups ('the big four'), the principal companies within an area were amalgamated and smaller companies absorbed. The Act came into being on 1 January 1923, and the branch line to Lee-on-the-Solent together with all the outstanding debts (then standing at £14,000 *[£642,000]*) was taken over by Southern Railways, no doubt to the relief of the board of directors of Lee-on-the-Solent Light Railway, which held its last ever board meeting at that time to approve the take-over. Needless to say, Southern Railways was not happy about being forced to take over the ailing company and its debts and it is little wonder that it immediately petitioned the Railway Amalgamation Tribunal in an attempt to avoid responsibility for the deficit. The Board did not approve the submission and Southern Railways appealed, only to lose once again.

In the meantime, even an improved service under Southern control did not solve the problem of small passenger numbers. It was still not possible to get a through-train to London, and the three Halts were closed from 28 April 1930. Eight months later, on 31 December 1930, the passenger service ceased altogether with the running of the 3.50pm train from Lee-on-the-Solent to Fort Brockhurst Station. The closure of the service was met with some indifference, as a report appearing in *The Portsmouth Evening News* of the following day shows:

Six Lee-on-the-Solent men and a dog travelled on the light railway from Lee to Fort Brockhurst ... with first class tickets on Wednesday, to mark the occasion of the last passenger train on regular service on this branch line.

The passengers waved to all and sundry as they journeyed along, and onlookers probably wondered what all the fuss was about, maybe forgetting that the day was the finishing day for the service. The young men also sang old time-songs. When nearly home the party was surprised to hear three loud reports as the train passed along the metals. Fog signals had been placed on the line by way of a farewell salute.

Handshaking all round took place when the train came to a standstill. Stationmaster, guard, engine-driver and fireman joined in and the best of good wishes were expressed, including that of "A happy and prosperous New Year".

It is pleasing to note that the officials displaced at Lee are already allotted positions elsewhere within the Railway Company.

A goods service to Lee-on-the-Solent was retained until 30 September 1935, but it was not a regular service and the trains operated on an 'as required' basis. Notwithstanding this official closure date for goods traffic, there was a last goods train on Wednesday 2 October 1935. Once again the local newspapers reported the occasion when *The Hampshire Telegraph* commented, on Friday 4 October:

So far as the railway is concerned, Lee-on-the-Solent is now "off the map". No more will the echoes resound with the shriek of the whistle and the popping of the fussy little engine which has daily dragged a goods train from Brockhurst to Lee and back again, for that goods train has left the quaint collection of buildings bearing the dignified title Lee Railway Station for the last time, carrying with it the safe, clock and other office furniture, as well as the station lamp and barrow.

For the last time, Mr. F.J. Marlow who for 13 years has been stationmaster, booking clerk, ticket collector, porter and lamp boy all rolled into one, locked the station doors, and joined Mr. M. Searle, Stationmaster at Gosport (whose administrative area includes Lee), and Mr. W. Foster, the guard, and made the journey to Brockhurst, at the end of a 16-truck train, in a brake van on Wednesday.

Mr. V.H. Bricknell, the engine driver, had been making the journey daily for 23 years. It fell to his lot to drive the last passenger train in 1930.

"We had a good service in the early days", he said, whilst "grooming" the engine, in preparation for his last journey. "I have known as many as 30 trains on a Bank Holiday. Things have changed". With a sad gesture he pulled out a piece of cotton waste, and wiped moisture from his hand.

But if he felt sad at this last phase of the change, he hid his feelings, for he tore the peace and quietude of Lee with a special fanfare on the engine whistle, and shattered it with a series of ear-splitting explosions from foghorn signals.

Thus closed a railway which has been in existence for nearly 45 years.

The track between Lee-on-the-Solent and Fort Gomer Halt was finally removed in 1939, although a half-mile stretch from Fort Brockhurst Station towards Fort Gomer Halt remained in use right up to 1955 for the delivery of coal supplies to Privett Farm owned by C H House & Sons Ltd.

7

ONE FOR THE ROAD

A map of 1791 (see Appendix 6) shows that there were no roads along the coast, east or west, to or from the hamlet of Lee Britten, the area which, within a hundred years, would be transformed by the arrival of the Robinson family to become Lee-on-the-Solent. On the ancient route from Titchfield to Gosport, at Stubbington, a road branched south to the coast. Where it reached the coast it was known as Stubbington Lane End, this being the site of the present western end of Marine Parade West where it turns north. Just under a mile to the east of the centre of Stubbington there was another road branching to the south, near the present-day Marks Road, and where a new entrance to the Daedalus site has recently been built. This ancient road passed Milwall Farm, (which later became known as Milville Farm), Court Barn and Lee Britten, ending up at the coast half a mile to the east of Stubbington Lane End. Midway between Milwall Farm and Court Barn the road forked to the South East, passing Shoot Farm and Chark Farm. It continued in a southerly direction until it reached Browndown in the area of the present-day traffic-light junction in Privett Road. Then it became a track which descended the slope near the junction and went across the Browndown rifle ranges, along the foreshore to near Gilkicker Point and then headed north to Alverstoke. Thus people travelling from Alverstoke to Stubbington by-passed Lee Britten. Interestingly this medieval route was to be followed centuries later by twenty-first-century road-builders when the current Lee by-pass, Cherque Way, was constructed in 2010.

When John Charles Robinson started the development of Lee-on-the-Solent, he obviously realised that he would need to be able

Manor Way (1893) which was one of the very few access roads to the area which became the new town

to transport building materials. He therefore had a road between Lee-on-the-Solent and Gosport constructed at his own expense. The route went across Browndown Common, which at that time was used for musketry practice by the marines and militia-men quartered in the barracks there. It ran from the end of Portsmouth Road, on the sea side of the main building of the Small Arms School, to join the road that ran from Privett to Stokes Bay at Gomer Corner, where the roundabout near Bay House School now stands. The road can still be seen alongside the present road, on the other side of the wire fence near the traffic lights at the end of Portsmouth Road. This became a military road in the Second World War and, in order to prevent public rights of way being acquired over it, was closed for one day each year.

Ironically, the road that John Charles Robinson had constructed was one of the factors that led to the demise of the railway, as it made it easier for the competition – in the form of the bus companies – to operate. By the 1920s Farelee Motors had established a motor-bus service between Fareham, Lee-on-the-Solent and Hill Head which ran daily half-hourly services in summer from 9am until 8.30pm.

An early motor bus service waiting outside Hannen's Private Hotel
(later Pier House), c.1912

Access to, and expansion of, the resort was always going to be a problem, which was exacerbated by the presence of the Browndown ranges to the east and, eventually, the Fleet Air Arm base to the west. When the Lee estate was bought by the Robinsons, access to it was thus somewhat limited. There was a medieval track from Stubbington, a rough road from Stokes Bay corner and a rough road on the path of the current Stubbington Lane.

A dispute over the access to Lee-on-the-Solent occurred as early as 1887. On 1 September of that year Mr C E Robinson sent a letter to the Fareham District Highway Board regarding "the obstructions at Court Barn." In the letter he points out that, at about the end of 1883, the Robinson family bought from Mr Delmé about 32 acres of land interspersed over the Lee estate, paying a high price at that time.

On 3 September 1884 a very successful sale of building land took place at Lee-on-the-Solent. Some of the land bought from Mr Delmé was included in the sale and fetched a higher price than was paid for it. This soured the relationship between the Robinson family and Mr Delmé and he sent them a letter through his solicitors intimating that, in the absence of an agreement, "no privileges" were to be exercised by Mr Robinson on Mr Delmé's retained land. A request by the Robinson family for an explanation met with no reply.

For many years prior to the purchase from Mr Delmé, the two old gates in Milvil Lane (the chief approach to Lee-on-the-Solent from Fareham) had been out of repair and unused, and there was only one gate in Court Barn Lane, which was never locked. In October 1884 two new gates, much larger and heavier than the old ones, were suddenly erected across Milvil Lane. They had pointed palings, preventing people from getting over them, and were made to swing closed, so that no one could pass them in a carriage without getting down to hold the gates open. The words 'Milvil Farm' were painted on them in large letters, giving the impression to strangers that the road led nowhere else. About the same time, the old gate in Court Barn Lane was locked, and a new second gate was put up there. A dangerous nuisance was thus created in Milvil Lane while the public were altogether *debarred from using Court Barn Lane except on foot only*.

In his letter Mr C E Robinson goes on to inform the Board that, when complaint was made to Mr Delmé, a reply was received to the effect that he (Delmé) fully endorsed the action of his agent, a Mr Giffiths, who had introduced the obstructions. As a consequence the dispute went to Winchester Quarter Sessions, not as a private action for damages, but for the obstruction of public highways.

At the same time the public soon found what a nuisance the obstructions were and sometimes forcibly expressed their disgust by damaging the gates. Mr Griffiths, in reply, went on to impute that the damage to the gates was at the instigation of Mr C E Robinson.

At the Quarter Sessions a compromise had been agreed between both parties, with the approval of the Judge, whereby all indictments were to be withdrawn, the Court Barn gates were to remain locked, the Milvil Lane gates were to be removed completely and Mr Robinson was to pay Mr Delmé £350 *[£29,500]*. Additionally each party was to defray its own costs. The Robinson family agreed to this rather expensive compromise as they felt it was in the public interest and that it was more important that Milvil Lane should be free from all impediments, rather than Court Barn Lane being opened as a carriageway. Two points of importance in the compromise were that: (1) the Court Barn gates which were to remain were to be only five-bar gates which anyone could get over and would not completely obstruct the footway, and (2) the compromise was binding on both parties and should not in any way obstruct the public.

The letter to the Board went on to say that Mr Griffiths had been "uttering falsehoods" to the effect that Mr Robinson had, through others, constantly annoyed the Court Barn tenant and destroyed her gates and also claimed that "the labour for removing the fences etc, had been provided by Mr. Robinson". The letter went on: *The fact is that it is Mr. Delmé's party who have broken the compromise, by repeatedly obstructing Court Barn Lane with nails and pointed rails on the gates, by digging ditches and felling trees across the road, and even putting up fences studded with tenter-hooks* [hooks or bent nails that hold cloth on a tenter or drying rack] *and tarred, to the general danger and inconvenience (of the public).*

Mr C E Robinson went on to say that the public were incensed and, although he sympathised with those who had taken the law into their own hands, he could not countenance their action which had resulted in the Highways Board becoming involved in the dispute following also the involvement of the parish vestry (local church representative). He said that the case had long since ceased to be a private matter.

At the Board hearing Mr Carter, the Surveyor, thought that the road should be maintained in its past condition and that it should be left to the public to assert their right as to carriages. Evidence of long-term local residents was heard. One man said that for 48 years he had known the lane and had never seen any stoppage in it at all. He considered it as much a carriageway as a footpath, but knew nothing about the repairs. A second man said he had lived for 47 years at Titchfield and had never known anybody interfered with when going through the lane. Other evidence showed that no difficulty existed before the Lee-on-the-Solent dispute.

The decision of the Board was that the highway should be maintained for foot passengers through Court Barn Road, but it would take no further action if Mr Delmé removed the obstructions, and paid the Board's costs.

Access via Milvil Lane was once again to become a bone of contention some 60 years later. During the Second World War, the Admiralty closed the roads associated with the medieval track that led from Milvil Road to Marks Road in Stubbington. After the War there was great concern by traders and inhabitants alike about the difficulty of getting in and out of Lee-on-the-Solent. The rail link had gone and newspaper quotes illustrate the problems faced in the post-war years. In December 1947 it was reported that *the Admiralty plans to keep permanently closed the four roads and three footpaths which had been closed at the outbreak of the Second World War especially as now part of Milvil Lane has been incorporated into the runway*".

Nothing seemed to be forthcoming except vague promises, and traders were becoming increasingly concerned, as this item of news in January 1950 illustrates: *Lee Chamber of Trade stated that "Except for the tenuous road from Gosport and the narrow Stubbington Lane, Lee is cut off from Fareham and the main road to the West. Their anxiety is to see the proposed road along Manor Way to Fareham constructed at the earliest possible moment.*

The local Member of Parliament, Dr Reginald Bennett, raised a question with the Minister of Transport regarding the Lee main road on 27 March 1950. It had previously been pointed out that the main road from Lee to Fareham had been closed early in the War to provide for aerodrome expansion. He then went on to enquire what were the plans regarding its replacement. It was recorded in *Hansard* as:

Road, Lee-on-Solent

27 March 1950

Surgeon Lieut.-Commander Bennett *asked the Minister of Transport if he has yet come to a decision about the proposals submitted to him for an alternative main road from Lee-on-Solent as replacement for that road closed by the Admiralty during the war.*

Mr. Barnes: *The county council have submitted proposals for the replacement of the closed road. I regard these as generally satisfactory, but the cost, which is estimated at £90,000 [£2,480,000], seems too large an expenditure to be incurred in present economic conditions, particularly as there is already an alternative route. I consider, however, that a new alternative road should be provided as soon as the economic situation permits.*

Surgeon Lieut.-Commander Bennett: *While thanking the Minister for his reply, may I ask if he has in mind the continuing waste which is being brought about by the diversion of traffic from the north and east through the village of Stubbington, north-west of Lee-on-Solent, and also the congestion and danger on this inadequate road? Is he also aware that the prolongation of this road's closing is handicapping a seaside resort, one of whose greatest assets should be its accessibility?*

Mr. Barnes: *Yes, sir. As I have already indicated, I do not consider the alternative road satisfactory, but in view of the restrictions on capital expenditure I regret that this is not possible at present. Its urgency and needs are, however, fully recognised.*

In February 1951 Lee's Manor Way scheme was postponed indefinitely. At that same time the road to Gosport continued to be a source of problems as two news items illustrate. In December 1953: *When a Naval Avenger aircraft was being transported on an articulated lorry it caused long delays especially when it became wedged near the entrance to Western Way in Alverstoke. It then caused further delays on Portsmouth Road in Lee.* In June 1955: *Mrs. Myrtle Michell of "Morning Light" Milvil Road fell from her motorbike along Browndown Road near the Stokes Bay Caravan Camp, she was taken to the Royal Hospital Portsmouth.*

The road at this time was in a poor state of repair with numerous potholes and damage caused by military vehicles such as tanks and 'alligators'. These were caterpillar-tracked amphibious vehicles similar to the wheeled-version Ducks (DUKWs) used in the D-Day landings and many were concealed in the grounds of the present Bay House School at that time.

There were many other road problems in the area. Stokes Bay Road had been closed during the war, and after hostilities ended, there was an agreement between the War Department (as the Ministry of Defence was then known) and Gosport Borough Council to a partial opening of that road from 1pm on Saturdays until lighting up time, and from 8am until lighting up time on Sundays and public holidays, with a speed limit imposed of 10mph. Where the Kingfisher caravan park is now sited was then a much lower marsh area. News reports of October 1952 show that: *Gosport Borough Council granted permission to raise land on Browndown marshes by controlled tipping of refuse.*

A little later the local MP was again asking questions in the House of Commons about the problems concerning the roads. This was reported in *Hansard* as:

Road, Gomer – Browndown

29 April 1955

Dr. Bennett *asked the Secretary of State for War if he is aware of the condition of the military road through Gomer and Browndown between Gosport and Lee-on-the-Solent; if he will institute repairs and the filling of pot-holes at the earliest possible opportunity; and if he will restore the road, especially at the sides, to a safe condition.*

Mr. Head: *This road has been adequately maintained for limited military purposes. I understand, however, that nine out of every ten of the vehicles using it are civilian, and we are, therefore, negotiating with the local authority for its handover.*

Relief eventually came with the construction of Broom Way, as it opened up a third road in to and out of Lee, and later in the 1960s, the extension of Privett Road along the route of the former railway to join up with Portsmouth Road was completed.

8

TRADESMEN'S ENTRANCE

The Robinsons had begun the process of establishing the resort by providing the infra-structure of roads, road and rail connections, water, drainage and sewerage disposal, gas and electric supplies (although electric street lighting would not be introduced until after the Second World War). Now it was time for the entrepreneurial tradesmen to enter the scene in the form of grocers, greengrocers, butchers, bakers and dairy merchants. Coal merchants, hardware merchants, wine merchants and the like were soon to follow.

On one of the very first plans to be drawn up for John Robinson in 1884, showing the proposed layout of the whole town, there is a large area reserved as a permanent market arcade. This shows two rows of 13 tiny plots each facing one another across a central open walkway. The site is located halfway between Pier Street and Beach Road and runs north-south between the High Street and Marine Parade East. While this feature never materialised once the development of the town commenced, it does at least show that there were very definite proposals from the outset for the accommodation of commercial premises near the seafront.

In the first five or six years of the existence of Lee-on-the-Solent, there were almost no establishments supplying provisions in the area other than the old local farms. By 1891 the only persons bearing any resemblance to what we might now consider to be shopkeepers were George Love, who was a baker and grocer at 1 Gosport Road and George Queary, who was a sub-postmaster living at 2 Pier Street, although at that time the Sub-Post Office business was conducted at the Pier Toll House during the day only. By the start of the twentieth century, however, purpose-built shops began to appear.

One of the most prominent among the pioneer tradesmen was Frederick Bulson, who was born in Jersey in 1859. He and his wife, Martha, who had also been born in Jersey, had run a tailor's business for a number of years in Islington before moving to Lee-on-the-Solent in 1897, when they set up their drapery business at Manor House on the corner of Manor Way and the High Street. Two of their sons, Percival and Clarence, assisted them and opened a grocery side of the business. Within a few years the family had acquired many of the adjoining commercial premises in the block and extended their business emporium to include outfitting, hosiery, stationery, grocery, hardware, china, boots, confectionery and tea-rooms under the trade name of 'F. Bulson's Stores and Pleasure Retreat'. The family maintained a flagpole outside on which the Union Flag was a regular sight.

Frederick Bulson, who later became a local councillor, was quick to realise the profits to be made from parties visiting the new resort. In a brochure of 1905 he advertised his Retreat as offering *accommodation to seat 400 children inside and 200 in a large marquee attached. Being a Superintendent of Sunday Schools for a number of years I know the objection teachers have to taking children to any place where a licence is held – for this reason I have built my retreat.* Another example of his advertising can be seen in the Personal column of *The Portsmouth Evening News* of Saturday 28 May 1904:

F. Bulson's Retreat, Lee-on-the-Solent, for Sunday Schools, Temperance Societies, mothers' meetings, etc.: special cheap railway fares for parties, now booking dates. Write for price list.

Earlier that year, on Thursday 31 March, the same column carried the following entry:

Dear Ada, Meet me at P. Bulson's Tea Rooms, High street, Lee-on-the-Solent on Easter Monday. We can get a nice plain tea for 6d [£2.09] but with two kinds of cake 9d [£3.14]. Take train from Gosport to Fort Brockhurst, then on to Lee.

Was this a tryst? We can only speculate as to reason why the author of this note did not use the postal system for the communication and will never know whether Ada did in fact turn up!

Bulson's Stores on the corner of High Street and Manor Way, c.1912

Besides Bulson's, the only other business in the High Street at the start of the twentieth century was at No 3, where Joseph King – an elderly widower – ran a confectioner's and baker's. The remaining few shops were concentrated on the eastern side of Pier Street. At No 1 was a grocer's owned by Henry Watts, and at the same premises there was a butcher's which was run by Henry's brother, George Watts. At No 2 was the Sub-Post Office, where Miss Rosina Queary had taken over from her father, George Queary. At No 3 Mr Frederick Hannen, former proprietor of the Victoria Hotel, ran a dairy business and a milk delivery service. He would later open a restaurant at these premises. At No 5 Miss Florence Coates was the manageress of a bakery and confectioner's.

Napoleon I once said that "England is a nation of shopkeepers" which he claimed was not meant as a disparaging comment, but merely a statement of fact. To some extent this would appear to be true locally, by the way in which the number of shops rapidly increased in Lee-on-the-Solent. At the same time that the development of the shops in the High Street and Pier Street was taking place, corner shops in other parts of the village became established. George Love's bakery and a grocery shop at No 1 Gosport Road (at the junction with Cambridge Road) was still trading and he had been joined in the business by his son, who bore the unusual name of Elberta. At No 1 House Cottages, Levi May conducted his business as a coal merchant and at No 1 Elmore Field, Edward Robinson was trading as a master tailor.

Most of the businesses in the village would provide a delivery service to the big houses, all of which would have two gates. One of these gates would have had a path that led to the side or back of the premises and that gate would be clearly labelled 'Tradesmen's Entrance'.

As the resort developed, the shops expanded in number and variety and many changes were seen. Whereas during the first few decades the Bulson family had increased its presence by opening more shops and a tea-room in the same section of the High Street, this 'empire' eventually declined until, by the end of the 1930s, it had returned to being a single grocery store. In February 1947 *The Hampshire Telegraph and Post* noted: *The funeral of Lee tradesman. Lee-on-the-Solent has lost a well known tradesman with the death of Percy Bulson (65) he carried on the business of grocer and provisions merchant founded by his father in 1897.*

By the 1930s the High Street and Pier Street had become the central shopping area of Lee-on-the-Solent and in 1936 the Lee-on-the-Solent Business Association was formed. By the outbreak of the Second World War, the number of shops in the High Street had increased to over forty. Among these were Smith Brothers' Garage, the Gosport District Gas Company showroom and two tea-rooms – namely 'Hove-To' on the corner of Milvil Road (which was patronised mainly by residents from the western end of Lee-on-the-Solent) and 'Rosemary Tea-Rooms' further down the High Street (mainly frequented by residents from the other end of town). The 'Hove To' tea-rooms also had an adjoining tea garden and pleasure grounds and at one time even boasted a tennis court for the benefit of their patrons. The premises were later demolished and replaced by a block of flats named Hove Court.

Further along the High Street there were two grocers, plus a Lipton's and a Co-op grocery stores, three butchers and a cold meat shop, a fish shop, a greengrocers, a bakery, a wine merchant, two dairies and two chemists. In 1933 Leonard Miles started a small lending library in his florist's shop at No 142 High Street and, later that year, he changed the whole business into a bookshop. This is now one of the very few businesses from that time which still trades today from the same premises, albeit under different ownership.

The shopping centre extended into Pier Street (which is now part of a local conservation area) and around the corner to include Marine Court Mansions, the Art Deco block built at the same time as the Tower and facing it across Marine Parade West. On the eastern side of Pier Street at around this time there was Bell's café, restaurant and boarding house; a newsagent; Lloyds Bank and Talbot & Co, estate agents. On the opposite side of the road, in the newly constructed Art Deco building, was Barclays Bank, a ladies' hairdresser, two estate agents, Bull's hardware store, a butcher's shop, a stationer's and Browning's bakery. Around the corner in Marine Court Mansions and facing the sea was the Post Office and the Electricity Board showroom and beyond the end of this building, on the corner of Milvil Road and Marine Parade West, was located the Bluebird Café. In the late 1940s this was second only to the Tower as the chief assembly-point for teenagers and was basically just a hut with a veranda. Later it became an American-style ice-cream parlour which, in summer had tables outside with brightly coloured sunshades. Most importantly, in the late 1950s and early 1960s, it had a juke-box and so it is no surprise that the café became a popular haunt of the young motorcycle- and scooter-riders of that time.

In addition to the increase in the number of shops in the main shopping area, there were more corner shops throughout Elmore. In some of the roads there was a gathering of these small shops to form satellite shopping areas. By the mid 1930s No 1 Gosport Road had become a boot repair shop, No 10 was Scott's general store and Bugg's grocery called 'Elmore Cash Store'. In Portsmouth Road, facing the Inn by the Sea, and starting at the top of the slope, No 174 was Reed's the chemists, then at No 172 was Moss fishmongers, at No 170 was the Sub-Post Office where Mr Agutter was the sub-postmaster, and at No 168 on the corner of Raynes Road was Rodd's grocery store. On the corner of Portsmouth Road and Elmore Road was Downing Garages, which has remained a garage premises up to the present day. 'Cornerways' tea-room, which was owned and run by the Misses Triggs, who baked delicious cakes and scones, was on the corner of Queen's Road and Portsmouth Road and faced Downing Garages. The property was built in 1934 and proved to be a popular venue for servicemen and women during the Second World War. No 7 Elmore Road, facing Seymour Road, was a grocery store run by Mrs Minnie Kingdon.

Although nearly all of the establishments have changed ownership or function over the years, some of the names associated with shopping in Lee-on-the-Solent in earlier times are worth recalling. The Bulson family name is remembered by some of the senior citizens who live, or have lived, in Lee-on-the-Solent, although the memories may not necessarily be confined to the grocery business or the tea-rooms. One well-known member of this family was Ronald David Bulson, son of Percival Bulson, who was born in 1919. He was known for his supposed invention of wooden swimming flippers for hands as well as feet and was sometimes to be seen swimming wearing a bowler hat, although it was never revealed if this was part of another invention. He also built the first catamaran to sail on the Solent. After the Second World War, in which he was first an ambulance driver for Civil Defence before working in RNAS at Priddy's Hard, he tried to run organised trips in a motor boat to the Isle of Wight. Originally this operated from the remains of the end of the pier accessed by the improvised pier erected just before D-Day, and later from a small jetty near the amusement arcade. It did not catch on and proved to be a short-lived venture. He was fiercely proud of his family and his home town of Lee and, towards the end of his life, he hand-typed his own, rather personal, history of Lee-on-the Solent of which he produced six copies and sent one to the Queen. He died in 1970, ending the Lee-on-the-Solent line of the family.

The Skipper family name is also well remembered. George Skipper established his garage business on the corner of Marine Parade East and Beach Road in the 1920s and it thrived right through until the 1960s. Old advertisements for the business proudly announce that it was agent for Humber, Hillman, Sunbeam and Commer. Both he and his wife, Gladys, were prominent and active members of the local community and were on the Board of Governors of Privett School. Mrs. Skipper was also a local town councillor for 20 years and was later made an honorary Alderman. In July 1951 she made an amusing observation to the Gosport Food Control Committee, which was reported in *The Hampshire Telegraph and Post*. At that time no offal was being allocated to Lee-on-the-Solent and Mrs Skipper, when talking about the slaughtered animals arriving at butchers in the town, commented that "they have no insides!" Some of the older residents will remember that in the summer months, Mrs Skipper was frequently seen with a very large shrimp net, her dress tucked into the bottom of the legs of her underwear (as was the custom), walking up and down in the shallow water off the beach opposite 'Skipper's Garage'. This was very much in keeping with her nature; she was not one to stand on ceremony, but was a very down-to-earth person.

Another long-term founding tradesman in the town who set up business just four years after the Bulsons was Mr Frederick Perkins. On 6 December 1946 *The Hampshire Telegraph and Post* reported the funeral of Mr Fredrick Perkins (63) of 148 Portsmouth Road, who had been in business in the High Street for 45 years as dairyman, caterer, and café proprietor.

One final well-known name to emerge in the early years of the town was that of Frederick R Flower who, in 1893, opened his estate agent's business. He came to Lee-on-the-Solent in 1907 and conducted his business from an office in the buildings which would become named after him on the sea side of Marine Parade. He also became a prominent member of the local Working Men's Club, a local councillor, school manager, assistant overseer, member of the Board of Guardians and was responsible for producing the early official guidebooks to Lee-on-the-Solent. His particular moment of glory came on the morning of Sunday 7 August 1921 when he was received by King George V and Queen Mary aboard the Royal Yacht at Cowes on which occasion, according to the reports, *the king expressed his great interest in Lee-on-the-Solent and its development*. Commemorative china cups were produced depicting this scene and one is still held by the Lee-on-the-Solent Working Men's Club. Frederick Flower retired in 1929 whereupon his business was taken over by Messrs Rackham & Vail.

9

BACK TO SCHOOL

Trafalgar House School and Wykeham Hall

One of the first buildings to appear along Marine Parade in the very early days of the development of the town was a large property on the corner of what is now Marine Parade East and Pier Street. The 1891 census shows that this was originally a private residence occupied by Mr Sholto Middleton, a retired schoolmaster and clerk in holy orders, with his wife, family and servants. Shortly afterwards Mr William Henry Webb, who had enjoyed a successful teaching career at Surbiton in Surrey, took over the building and opened it as Trafalgar House School on 6 May 1892.

The new establishment was advertised as a "High Class School for the sons of Gentlemen" and prepared boys for various public examinations. The subjects taught included elementary science, shorthand, algebra, Euclid, French and Latin.

In 1895 the school moved to a newly constructed and rather imposing building, which would later become

Trafalgar House School on the corner of Pier Street and Marine Parade East, 1894

known as Wykeham Hall, at the junction of King's Road and Norwich Place, and the old school building was taken over by Lee College (see below). Initially the name of Trafalgar House School was retained after the move. Adjoining the new premises was a large cricket field, also owned by Mr Webb, which provided a very useful school facility.

Mr. Webb was joined at the school by Mr G E Oxley MA, who had moved from Bexley Heath College in Kent, and the two became joint principals. They advertised over a wide area and, in 1901, announced: *During the past three years, out of a large number sent up for various Public Examinations, there have only been two failures... The School Building has been erected especially for its purpose within 3 minutes of the Sea. Each Boy has a separate cubicle. There is a large garden, and a playing field of 5 acres attached to the School.*

Oxley does not appear to have been at the school very long and Webb left to return to teaching in Surbiton in 1903. Webb's son, Ernest William Webb, then became the school's headmaster and around this time the name of the school was changed to Wykeham Hall. The 1911 census shows that, in addition to Ernest, his wife Agnes and their two children, there were 26 pupils in residence, a matron and seven servants. Things were set to change some years later when, in 1916, the family made national news. The story is best summarised by one news report of the time from as far away as Scotland (*Dundee Courier*, Wednesday 8 March 1916). Under the rather lengthy headline: '*You have been a ripping husband to me'— is wife's somewhat inconsistent admission on running away to live with doctor.* The item continued:

In the Divorce Court yesterday, before Mr. Justice Horridge and a common jury, Mr. Ernest William Webb schoolmaster, of Wickham [sic] Hall, Lee-on-the-Solent was granted decree nisi on the ground of his wife's misconduct with Dr. Lewis Walker, of Lee-on-the-Solent, against whom the jury assessed damages of £2,000 [£109,000].

Parties lived on affectionate terms until April, 1914. Petitioner was friendly with Dr. Walker, who sent one of his sons to petitioner's school. On April 9, the wife wrote a letter to the petitioner containing the words:- 'I have gone away with Dr. Walker, and so shall never return. You have been a ripping husband to me and I am truly sorry. I never loved you as I have loved him.You won't want scandal for the sake of the children. Forget me as soon as you can. I am sorry I treated you like this'.

Petitioner replied:- 'Oh, my poor kid. How could you do such a thing. The worst of it is that it is irremediable now. I am a bit stunned, and I do not quite know what I am doing. I will divorce you so that you can marry Walker. I loved you so much, kid.'

In 1917 the Admiralty requisitioned Wykeham Hall as part of the programme of development of the air base at Lee-on-the-Solent. The building became the Officers' Mess and later served as a major Fleet Air Arm HQ. Webb moved his school once again and rented Seafield Park on the Fareham edge of the airfield and changed the name of the school to match the location. In autumn 1916 he married Minnie Louisa Flint and in 1923 transferred the ownership of the school to her.

History repeated itself at the outbreak of the Second World War when, once again, the Admiralty requisitioned the school premises for use as a barracks and signal school. The school had to move and went to Endsleigh House, Milton Abbott, near Tavistock in Devon. At the end of the War it was not possible for the school to return, as the Admiralty retained the use of Seafield Park and then purchased the property. Capt. Hope-Lang became the headmaster in 1946 and the school moved to Lower Beeding in Sussex and became known as Newells and then Handcross Park School, under which name it still exists.

Edinburgh House School

This school was founded by Mr William H Colborne and Mr James Cruickshank MA in 1895 on the eastern side of Manor Way as a preparatory school for boys up to the age of 14 and specialised in preparing them for the Royal Navy and for public schools. Mr Colborne had been born in Gosport and was the vice-principal of Eastman's, a well-known school in Southsea, before his appointment as vice-principal of Eastman's RN Academy in Fareham. Mr. Cruickshank was a native of Scotland and came to Lee-on-the-Solent in 1891. He had gained considerable experience in preparing boys for Army examinations and, for over four years prior to opening the school in Lee, had been preparing pupils for Naval Cadetships. He was also an active member of the Parish Council and a founder member of the Lee Golf Club (see Chapter 25). The new school was often called 'The Royal Naval School' and the principals regularly placed advertisements for it in the Education columns of *The Hampshire Telegraph*, *The London Standard* and *The Morning Post*.

Following the deaths of William Colborne in 1907 and James Cruickshank in 1926, the school was carried on by the latter's widow, Louisa, her son Stuart Colborne Cruickshank MA (prizeman of Clare College, Cambridge) and Mr E Kingsley Kefford MA (of St John's College, Cambridge). By the time they took over, some 650 boys had passed through the school. At this time the school had grown and occupied four large detached houses, all connected by corridors. Additionally there were playing fields at the rear, an enclosed gravel playground, gymnasium, recreation room, library, tuck shop and hobby rooms. The domestic arrangements were supervised by Mrs Louisa Cruickshank assisted by two matrons; a night porter was employed and not more than four boys were allocated to any one dormitory. The fees for boys under the age of ten were 90 guineas *[£4,550]* per annum and 95 guineas *[£4,800]* per annum for those over the age of ten.

Edinburgh House School in Manor Way, 1927

The school prospectus issued around 1927 provided a summary of the school day:

7.40am	Get up
8.10am	Prayers
8.15am	Breakfast
9.00am-11.15am	First School
11.15am-11.45am	PT & Break
11.45am-1.10pm	Second School
1.15pm	Lunch
1.45pm-2.15pm	Rest
2.15pm-4.30pm	Games
4.30pm-6.00pm	School
6.00pm	Tea
7.00pm-8.15pm	Prep
8.15pm	Supper & Prayers
8.30pm	Bed

(Small boys went to bed at 7.00pm and, during summer, afternoon work began at 2.15pm with games at 3.45pm)

A half-day holiday was given every Wednesday and Saturday; all boys assembled for morning and evening prayers and attended parish church on Sundays.

The subjects taught were Latin, French, Mathematics, English, History, Geography and Scripture. Greek or German were taught "when required". The classes were kept small so that each boy could receive full attention and each subject period lasted for 45 minutes. In summer the games activities included cricket (matches were arranged), athletics (annual sports days were held halfway through the summer term) and swimming in the sea at Lee (every boy was taught to swim before leaving the school and individual swimming championships and races were held). In winter there was football and boxing (boxing championships for four challenge cups were held annually).

The dining room of Edinburgh House School, 1927

Every boy did one hour of Physical Training (PT) per week and, in winter, 45 minutes on gymnasium apparatus. Each boy was given a PT exercise book setting out all the breathing and body exercises required. A copy of this survives and commences with the exhortation "Trumpet vigorously to clear the nostrils" and ends with advice on leading a healthy life, such as "Seek natural relief daily as early, punctually and regularly as possible" and also "Breathe as much as possible only through the nose, especially in east winds"!

The school community was divided into four 'houses' or 'sets' – wasps, birds, knights and frogs – and a challenge cup was awarded at the end of each term for the set which had gained the most points for work and games.

While most of the facilities appear to have been readily provided by the school (even down to two newspapers in the library each day) the School Prospectus does state that *On joining each boy is expected to bring two pairs of sheets, four pillow cases, six towels, a dessert spoon and teaspoon, and a dessert and table fork.*

The common room of Edinburgh House School, 1927

We can also get an insight into life at the school from the perspective of a schoolboy. Harry Ronald Taylor joined the school in September 1915 and remained there until Easter 1919. During that time he kept a diary, which has survived, and this provides some interesting comments of which the following are a selection:

Summer Term 1916

This term I first saw a boatplane.

Christmas Term 1916

This term a most important event occurred...in which I suffered the cane. We stuck up placards all over the school and unfortunately I forgot to haul mine down and suffered punishment from the Boss [the headmaster].*Which I assure the reader did not hurt much.*

Also one pupil ran away but was *hauled back by Mr. Ashton (who now has a false leg).*

A smoking row occurred this term, my brother was in this but not prominent.

This term a Zeppelin adventured over Lee way but I woke up in the middle and thought it was gun practice so went back to sleep again.

Mrs. Luckins (a well-known Lee inhabitant) had her periodical fit of madness and eventually was carted off to Fareham but now is back again.

Easter Term 1917

I remember a well known Sunday this term in which Mr. Thiérry [one of the schoolmasters] *took us for a walk to the butts. We all gathered up bits of lead and eventually the old keeper with a gun came and marched Watts off. Thiérry meanwhile was along the beach with the rest of the school. We hailed him back and gave chase to the old johnny. Eventually we reached him and got poor Watts (who was in a blue funk) released.*

During this period there was a vast craze ... for model wooden aeroplanes...they were very well made.

Lee gun was put into action for practice this term but is now useless at Elmore.

Summer Term 1917

Butterfly craze was very frequent during the summer term of this period.

Christmas Term 1918

Armistice Day was signed at 5.30 November 11 1918. I remember this day well how I went with Stuart Cruickshank [a fellow pupil and later co-principal of the School] *on his bike (adorned with flags) to the RFC* [Royal Flying Corps] *'drome where they were sending up rockets.*

School concert — me as Jane the maid.

Easter Term 1919

... a house which caught fire and made a terrible blaze and aroused the spirits of the pupils.

A curious paper chase from Edinburgh House School to Gomer and back — came off quite successfully.

Wright boarded the RNAS [Royal Naval Air Service] *motor boat when it was attached to the pier. Alas! The rope broke away from the pier — Motor boat starts to go out — all hands to the rescue. We get the rope after he has had half a dozen shots at the hook. RNAS men return — scold him. They go. Few days later Wright scales the pier underneath — very dangerous. Going on pier forbidden.*

Myself, Adams and Terry went out in boat from Hill Head and investigated the Haven Harbour.

Taylor seems to have enjoyed his days at the school as, at the end of his diary, he writes:

Since I have been at Edinburgh House I have had the pleasure of being under the following masters:-

Mr. Ingram (now at another school)

Mr. Ashby (now having a false leg)

Mr. Tatham (sports master)

Mr. Woods (a mistake!)

Mr. Thiérry (a Frenchman)

Mr. Martin (Ecclesiastes!)

Mr. Hughes (demobilised from RNVR)

Mr. Wall (a very decent chap, good boxer and gym master)

Mr. Cohen (a friend of my mater)

The following mistresses have been in the school during my time: Mrs. Armstrong, Miss White, Miss Yonge (1) and Miss Yonge (2)

J. Cruickshank (was the headmaster, very brainy old man, liked very much).

Edinburgh House School remained at Lee-on-the-Solent until 1939, when the premises were requisitioned by the Admiralty as accommodation for WRNS. After several moves during the War (to Wellington in Somerset and Brightwell Baldwin in Oxfordshire) the school finally moved to the Great Ballard site at New Milton in 1946. It amalgamated with Gorse Cliff School and Marchwood Park School in 1969 and, in 1995, joined with Fernhill Manor School to form The Ballard Schools. The junior school, Ballard Lake Preparatory School, remains on the Edinburgh House School site in New Milton. The original detached houses occupied by the school in Manor Way at Lee-on-the-Solent remain and are now private residences.

Lee College and St Boniface School

Unlike the other schools mentioned so far, this establishment catered exclusively for girls for most of its time in Lee, although it did start to take some boys onto the register towards the end. It was founded in Lee-on-the-Solent in the early / mid 1890s by Alice Ada Adamson who had moved from Greenwich, where she had been a school governess. She was assisted by her sisters Frances, Ellen and Olive, and often the school register comprised not only local pupils but also boarders from British families resident in India. The ages of the pupils generally ranged from 7 to 14.

In 1895 the school took up occupation of the premises on the corner of Marine Parade East and Pier Street which had been vacated by Trafalgar House School (see above).

While the school provided general education, it specialised in music, dance and drama. The list of staff included a 'music professor', and a French governess as well as other teachers. Miss Olive Anderson was herself an accomplished musician. It was a successful establishment and an insight into its activities can be gleaned from a short item appearing in *The Portsmouth Evening News* of Saturday 9 April 1904:

The annual concert by the pupils of Lee College was given in the Hall, Lee-on-the-Solent, on Wednesday. The performers acquitted themselves with their usual efficiency. A varied programme was presented, which consisted of vocal and instrumental music and recitations. A graceful dance and an Irish dance in costume proved most attractive items. A somewhat ambitious undertaking was the rendering of Franklin Taylor's "Toy Symphony". The Rev. R.E. Leigh, Vicar of Crofton, presented the prizes to the fortunate recipients, and the certificates which had been obtained from the Trinity College of Music and Cambridge local during the past year.

In 1907 the school transferred to a couple of large detached houses in Marine Parade West and in about 1931, during the time that Miss McLellan was the principal, the name was changed to St Boniface School. Miss Winifred Bennett became joint principal in about 1932 and the two ladies were assisted by a staff of fully qualified mistresses and visiting 'professors'. Pupils were both local and boarders and the school prepared them for all the recognised public examinations. The facilities at the school buildings included hard- and grass-courts on which lacrosse, netball and tennis were played. Swimming lessons were also provided under the supervision of the resident games mistress.

St. Boniface School, Marine Parade West, c. 1910

Miss McLellan retired as joint principal around 1939 and, during the Second World War, the school was evacuated and the buildings requisitioned by the Admiralty for use as a sick bay. The staff and pupils returned to the buildings briefly in peacetime, until the school finally closed in 1950. During this time the schoolgirls were a familiar sight attending services at St Faith's Church, where they usually occupied the front two rows. Following closure, many of the pupils transferred to the Lee-on-the-Solent Primary (Junior) School and the buildings were acquired by Hampshire County Council for use as a children's home with comparatively little adaptation necessary. The original houses still remain but are now private residences.

Lee-on-the-Solent Junior School

The Lee-on-the Solent Council School opened on a site off Cambridge Road on 28 September 1908. It replaced an earlier temporary school building on the site which had catered for 97 children under just one teacher. When the new school opened there were 150 pupils on the register, with Miss Amelia Elvey as headmistress, a role in which she continued until ill-health forced her retirement in 1923. In 1925 an outbreak of diphtheria occurred at the school. Although only about four pupils were affected, the mere mention of the condition was enough to cause alarm. The school building originally comprised just three rooms, of which one was divided into two by a moveable partition which could be pulled back for assemblies and other special occasions.

Miss Amelia Elvey, headmistress of Lee Junior School from 1908-1923

71

In the 1930s and 1940s Mr Maurice E Nixon was the headmaster. Like many schoolteachers of his day, he had a propensity to use the cane when he felt circumstances required it but, despite this, he was a popular figure. He is remembered on one occasion for taking into the school a grass snake which he had caught locally. The pupils were encouraged to pass it round the class and see how smooth it was – an early 'hands-on' zoology lesson which one could not imagine being repeated nowadays. In the Second World War the school was evacuated, although not all of the pupils went away. For a short time after it was re-established in Lee, it was run from the upstairs of the local library. Also, during the War, an ambulance station was located near the main gate of the school. Two vehicles were used by the station, one of which was a Rolls Royce. After the War, the later headmasters included Mr A Ludlow Fisher up to 1958 and also Mr Basil A H Bird.

By 1954 the conditions at the school had become such that the Mayor of Gosport was prompted to write to the Hampshire Education Authority to draw to its attention the urgent need for extra classroom facilities. He reported it was the only school in the borough with a waiting list on which there were children who were more than six years old and that a situation existed whereby children were being kept at home who should be at school – and that those children attending had to put up with "appalling conditions". A few years before this, a scheme for additional accommodation and necessary furniture was ordered, but the Ministry – in curtailing its capital expenditure – placed a ban on the proposal. Fortunately the difficulties were eased when expansion was finally sanctioned.

The original school building remains and now houses three classrooms, the head and the deputy head teacher's offices, an activity room, workroom, staff room and kitchen. In 1968 the building was extended on the eastern end by the addition of a large hall which now also acts as the school dining room. A further extension beyond this was added in 1976 to provide further classroom accommodation. This part of the building is also now used for the school library. Behind the main building, a new block was built in 2003 to provide further classrooms. In addition to this expansion, the inside of the building has been much altered to meet the changing needs of the school.

The school now caters for pupils aged 7-11 in Years 3-6 and the total number of children on the school register is approximately 350. The grounds have extended eastwards over the years and now provide a school playing field as well as extensive playground facilities.

Lee-on-the-Solent Infant School

This school, located in Elmore Road, was established for pupils aged 5-7 in Reception and Years 1 and 2. The original school building was constructed in 1974 and catered for three class groups, totalling about 40 pupils within each year. When the number of children seeking admission to the school declined in the 1980s, the school reduced to two classes for each year.

A little later, the establishment of large housing developments in the town led to an increase in the demand for places at the school. Conditions had been attached to the grant of planning consents for such developments requiring builders to make a contribution towards the cost of expanding facilities within the infrastructure. By this means, part of the cost of a building project at the school was financed and an additional infants' classroom, pre-school classroom and music room were provided. At the same time alterations were made to the entrance, office and staff room and a three-class system was once again established. The building works began in May 2004 and were completed in November 2005. More recently, in the summer of 2008, a new detached block for use as a children's centre was added at the side of the school.

The total number of children on the register is approximately 270 and the school enjoys landscaped grounds with courtyards and garden areas, together with a vegetable garden. The children assist with the maintenance of these areas as part of their schoolwork. The playing fields used by the school are located at the rear and are shared with the adjoining junior school.

10

SEE YOU IN CHURCH

St Faith's Anglican Church

To provide for the spiritual needs of the new population in the early days of the development of the resort, the Robinson family had reserved a central square of almost two acres (where St Faith's Church now stands) on which to build a church. It was intended that the land would be presented to the townspeople as a gift as soon as a permanent church had been built. Until building work began, it was necessary to make a temporary arrangement. Around 1894, Sir John Robinson purchased a small iron church for £20 [£1,630] and had it erected at his own expense. The church could seat a congregation of around 150 and the priest in charge from that time until his death in 1901 was Rev Edmund Davys. Sometimes the services were conducted by Mr Webb of Trafalgar House School (see Chapter 9). He held a Bishop's licence as a lay reader, but occasionally he would struggle to make himself heard above the noise of the rain on the metal roof during bad weather. A Sunday School was soon established which also provided children with outings to various local spots.

The small tin hut had a very useful and successful life and served the congregation for much longer than anyone at the time could have envisaged. It was not until 16 May 1932 that the foundation stone of the new St Faith's Church was laid in a ceremony presided over by Bishop Neville Lovett and the then parish priest, Rev Douglas Egbert Hunter, whose vicarage had been built in Richmond Road in 1929-30. The new church was erected right next to the old iron church so that there would be no interruption in the weekly services

Interior of St Faith's tin church, 1894

while building works proceeded. Architects John Seely and Paul Paget designed the new church and, when completed in 1933, it proved to be an impressive structure able to seat 400 people. The architectural historian Nikolaus Pevsner wrote of it that: *It is demure outside, rose-red brick walls, white framed windows, little bell cote over gable end, as if designed for a 'garden city'.*

The arches inside the church were cast *in situ* and are a striking feature of the design. The west window was donated by the Bishop of Winchester and dedicated to the memory of Theodore Woods, former Bishop of Winchester from 1924-1932. Originally it had been intended that the window would be installed at the Chapel of Winchester College, but plans were changed as a result of the Second World War and it was later adapted to fit into the new church. The cost of the new building was £10,188 *[£570,000]* and, when it was dedicated by Bishop Lovett on 21 June 1933, £2,000 *[£114,000]* was still outstanding and needed to be raised. Once services could be held in the new building, the old tin structure was finally removed.

In 1935 Lee-on-the-Solent became a separate parish and St Faith's became the parish church. From 1939-1946 the church was used by personnel from HMS Daedalus for their Sunday-morning parade services. As a mark of their thanks and appreciation they presented the church with a bell, which was dedicated in 1949 and now hangs at the west wall.

In February 1997, St Faith's Church was given Grade II listed building status by the Department of National Heritage.

In 1919, following the death of their three sons in the Great War, William and Ann Lowry decided to create a suitable memorial by buying land in High Street and erecting on it a former YMCA hut for use by the community. Photographs of their sons were hung on the walls inside the hut. The couple donated the land and the hut to St Faith's Church and the facility became a popular feature of the town, but it was always in need of much repair. In 1953 Gosport Borough Council approved a grant of £250 *[£5,600]* to the Parochial Church Council towards the costs of essential external repairs to the structure. By 1970, however, the hut was in a very poor state of repair once again and the Parochial Church Council decided to sell the land and use the proceeds to fund the building of a new hall adjacent to the church at Victoria Square. This new facility cost £35,000 *[£142,000]* and was opened as 'The Lowry Room' in November 1979.

By 1996 it was apparent that The Lowry Room was not big enough to cater for the expanding needs of the community and so the decision was made to add a further, larger hall as part of a new Parish Centre development. The foundation stone of the new development was laid on 25 June 1999 and the Centre was opened later that year at a cost of £365,000 *[£508,000]*. This was financed by various means including fundraising within the parish, a National Lottery grant of £66,500 *[£90,500]* and a bequest from a parishioner, Ronald Bulson (see Chapter 8), whose family name was used for the new hall – 'The Bulson Hall'. Although he was a keen parishioner, he did not always see eye to eye with the priest. One story relates how he once wrote a letter to the vicar, wrapped it in a brick and threw it through the vicarage window!

St John the Evangelist Roman Catholic Church

The land in South Place on which St John the Evangelist Church now stands was part of one of the plots sold off by Sir John Charles Robinson during the initial development of Lee. A Conveyance dated 1 October 1897 records that Sir John sold off that plot to one Edward Denham Tomlinson. Later the land came into the ownership of Miss Ethel Catherine Kilburn, who lived in 'White Cottage' in Portsmouth Road. She appears to have owned all of the land extending from South Place in the west to Ryde Place in the east and to Clifton Road in the north. During the Great War, Miss Kilburn approached Bishop Cotter of the Portsmouth Diocese and asked permission to erect an army hut on part of her land for use as a Catholic Church to enable Catholic prisoners of war to attend Mass. The first service held in the hut was in 1916, at which time it was served from Gosport parish and regular services were soon established.

By a Conveyance dated 17 September 1925 made between Miss Kilburn of the one part and four members of the Catholic Clergy (The Rt Rev Timothy Cotter, Bishop; The Rt Rev John Watson; The Very Rev John Henry King and the Very Rev Isidor Joseph Thomas Kuner) of the other part, Miss Kilburn generously donated the hut and part of her land to the Portsmouth Diocese. Thus was established the Parish Church of St John the Evangelist, Lee-on-the-Solent. The church was still served from Gosport, however, and would remain so until 1932, after which the parish priest of St John's was in residence in Lee, Gosport having no further connections with the Lee Parish except to send a supply priest when the Lee priest was absent.

During most of the Second World War the parish priest was Father John Feddis. He caused something of a stir among the older, more conservative members of the parish when they learnt that on Sunday afternoons he would not only allow the back garden of the presbytery to be used for games of football by the altar boys and any other interested parties, but often would also join in himself!

During the 1940s and 1950s one of the major ways of fund-raising within the parish was by way of a weekly football sweepstake called

'Pontoon' which was run by Lee and HMS Daedalus parishioners. A large part of the money raised was used for the building of a new church in Bridgemary in December 1954. The baptismal registers of Lee from this time show the wide geographical area ministered to by the parish priest, Father Michael Hennessy. Until the new church was built in Bridgemary, the Lee Parish extended to the west side of Gomer Lane in the east, northwards through the area which became Bridgemary Parish, and westwards across the area which later became Stubbington Parish. With such a large area to cover it is little wonder that, on some winter mornings, the congregation who were assembled and waiting at the church had to summon him from his bed because he had a tendency to oversleep.

Fr Hennessy died in 1977 and was succeeded by Fr Percy Collier. He immediately felt that the presbytery (which was then at 82 Portsmouth Road) was too large for someone who lived as simply as he did, so he moved to a smaller property at 6 Elmore Road. He was unable to drive or even ride a bicycle, so he walked everywhere in all weathers. If he accepted a lift from a parishioner it was because it gave him more time to see other parishioners. He was well-known and much liked throughout the area and left behind a great legacy of music and musicians. He played the organ and taught music – keyboard, recorder and flute, and continued teaching right up to his death in 1993.

Like its Anglican counterpart, the old 'temporary' church served the community well and for much longer than anyone might have envisaged. By the time Fr Percy Collier took over as parish priest it was clear that a new building was desperately required. It was not until three years later in 1980 that this materialised, when a new church was constructed on the site next to the old hut at a cost of £69,848.05 [£105,000]. The late Fr Hennessy had received a legacy of £30,000 [£45,200] on the death of his father and had put this aside towards the cost of building the new church.

The architects of the new church were Kanavan & Wingfield of Waterlooville and the builder was Cardesson Ltd also of Waterlooville.

Although some of the furnishings were transferred from the old church, parishioners and benefactors also donated many new items. On Christmas Day 1980, the first Mass was celebrated in the new church and on Tuesday, 19 May 1981 the solemn blessing and consecration of the building was conducted by Bishop Emery. The old asbestos hut was then demolished.

In the 1990s there was an increasing number of church and social functions within the parish and it become apparent that a church hall was badly needed. In 2002 an extension was incorporated onto the front of the church and this hall was formally opened by the parish priest of the time, Fr David Whitehead.

In 2003 the parish of Lee-on-the-Solent was merged with the parish of Stubbington. On 1 September 2010 the four parishes of Lee & Stubbington, Fareham & Portchester, Gosport and Park Gate were merged into one large parish of Our Lady Star of the Sea, Fareham & Gosport.

Methodist Church

Although the Methodist Church was not the first of the churches in Lee to be built, as the Anglican Church was originally using an older temporary building, it was the first permanent church to be built, making it the oldest.

The church, on the corner of Studland Road and High Street, occupies two of the original plots which were laid out when the resort was first divided up in the days of the Robinson Family. A Conveyance dated 30 April 1896 records that the north-western plot (being that half of the present site nearer to Studland Road) was sold by Sir John Charles Robinson to Harriett Brown. The other plot (now constituting the other half of the site) was sold by Sir John Charles Robinson, under a Conveyance of 18 November 1895, to Thomas Andrew Raynes who has already been mentioned above as one of the directors of the Lee-on-the-Solent Pier Company (see Chapter 5).

In 1897, William James Pyle of Wesley Lodge founded the Methodist Church on the site and the building was completed later that year. He had been born in Catherington in 1836 and moved to Fareham in the summer of 1858, establishing a business as a baker and confectioner in West Street. He became a prominent member of the newly established local Methodist Church and was appointed as the Sunday School Secretary or Superintendent, a post which he held for many years. A much-respected figure in the community, he later retired to Lee-on-the-Solent where he lived with his second wife, Ellen (née Cremer), whom he had married in 1885. She too, although deaf by that time, was an active member of the church, having been a founder member of the Sunday School in Fareham in 1859. She came from a devoutly religious Fareham family (her mother, Harriet Cremer, was a prominent member of the local Fareham Methodist Church, and her brother, William Randal Cremer, winner of the Nobel Peace Prize in 1903, had also been a Sunday School teacher before he moved to London in 1852). William and Ellen Pyle did much to ensure the efficient running and establishment of the new church in Lee up until their deaths. Ellen died in 1920 at the age of 82, and in 1926 William died at the grand age of 90. He was much missed in the community.

The building has remained a place of worship for Methodist congregations throughout and, in the 1930s, further building works were carried out on the High Street elevation to form a small church hall. These were extended later in 1957 with the foundation stones being laid on 6 February of that year. The hall is now used extensively by various local groups and is a popular venue for coffee mornings.

The Church That Never Was

On an early plan of the whole estate, drawn up in 1884 and showing the proposed layout of the entire town, a specific feature is made of Elmore Lake as the centrepiece of a large park. It rather looks as though the intention was to landscape the whole site. A number of footpaths are shown meandering through it and so there seems little doubt that this was to have been a major pleasure facility for the townspeople. At the western end of the 'park' and near the junction of Portsmouth Road and Marine Parade East there is the marking of "Church Site" which appears in addition to the "Church Site" marked in Victoria Square and upon which St Faith's Church was established. Neither the park nor the church at Elmore ever came to fruition, no further details can be identified regarding the proposed church and we can only speculate about it.

IIII

STAYING THE NIGHT

The Victoria Hotel

The Victoria Hotel was originally a remote farmhouse constructed in the seventeenth century with massive walls and oak floors and with a roof built around a large brickwork chimney in the old hamlet of Lee Britten. When the Lee-on-the-Solent Estates Company started the initial development of the resort in 1884, the building was modernised and converted into the town's first hotel. The application for the hotel licence was reported in *The Hampshire Telegraph* on Saturday 30 August 1884:

An application in respect of an hotel licence for this estate, which is in the course of development near Hill Head, Titchfield, was made by Mr. E. Goble. The applicant was Mr. Edmund Arthur Robinson of Lee House, Lee Lane, otherwise Manor Way, Lee-on-the-Solent, estate manager to Mr. John Charles Robinson, his father; and the licence applied for was in respect of the sale of all intoxicating liquors, to be consumed either on or off the premises. Mr. Goble said the premises for which the licence was required would be called the Victoria Hotel. He made the application with an immense amount of confidence.

He would draw...attention to the fact that the hotel was to be of a first class character, so as to provide a place of rest and retirement for overworked, professional men and others, moving in a high circle of society. Of course, there were many hotels at such places as Southsea, Ryde and Eastbourne, but the perfect rest which many visitors from London required was not to be obtained there.

The Chairman: Is the hotel built?

Mr. Goble: Yes, sir, and finished.

He then proceeded to refer to the high position held by Mr. Robinson, which was a guarantee that the hotel would be carried on in a first-class style.

It was absolutely necessary that there should be some hotel accommodation in the neighbourhood for the engineer and surveyor to the estate, as well as for others employed on it, and for those who visited the neighbourhood with the idea of purchasing the building land there. The laying out of the estate would confer an absolute benefit to the parish of Titchfield, because the rates would be decreased to a considerable extent by the buildings which were to be erected.

The nearest hotels were the Red Lion, at Stubbington, and the Osborne View, at Hill Head. These were about 1½ miles distant, and were of insufficient accommodation for those for whom it was intended to enter at the Victoria Hotel. Mr. Robinson had developed Swanage in the same way as he now proposed to develop the neighbourhood of Hill Head.

There appeared to be no objection to the licence on the part of the residents in the district, and no one was present to oppose the application.

The Magistrates retired for deliberation, and on their return into Court three-quarters of an hour later, the Chairman said they had given the case a very long and anxious consideration, because they felt the application to be of quite an exceptional nature. They were in this difficulty — on the one hand they were anxious not to throw cold water on a scheme that appeared to be a bona fide one, and might confer a benefit on the neighbourhood; but on the other hand they felt that if the scheme should not succeed they would have planted a licensed house in a neighbourhood almost uninhabited, which might very possibly prove anything but a benefit to the locality. However, after weighing the whole of the circumstances, they had determined to grant the licence with the understanding that, should the scheme fail, the Magistrates reserved to themselves the power of shutting up the house at any moment. He intimated the wish of the Bench that no bar should be provided at the hotel; and Mr. Goble said that this was also the desire of the owners.

Mr Frederick Hannen and his wife, Frances, took over as the first managers. Although relatively young (at ages 29 and 31 respectively) they were well-experienced in the hotel trade, having previously run the Dolphin Hotel in the High Street at Littlehampton in Sussex. They turned out to be successful entrepreneurs who put much of their personal energy into running the new hostelry and were usually assisted by a kitchen maid, a cook and a 'boots' boy. Frederick Hannen later served as a local councillor.

The establishment had five bedrooms for guests and some splendid fireplaces set with Dutch tiles portraying representations of biblical scenes. Outside it boasted an 'old world' garden at the rear with a tennis lawn and bowling green (first used on Whit Monday 1886). On the northern edge of the grounds there was a separate, panelled Assembly Room capable of accommodating up to 200 guests which, in addition to hosting auction sales of the early plots of land in the new development, was also used for concerts, dinners and balls.

The Victoria Hotel (now renamed The Bun Penny), 1894

It is clear from reading the various newspaper reports of the times that the Hannens worked closely with the Robinsons and the Estates

Company and that they could always be relied upon to 'put on a good spread' when it came to hosting official functions and entertaining visiting dignitaries.

By 1898 the couple decided that it was time to move on and branch out on their own, so they left the hotel and set up business at 3 Pier Street, where they ran a dairy and also opened a restaurant. At this point we leave the Hannens, but they will appear in this chapter once more a little later. The management of the Victoria Hotel was taken over by Henry William Smith and his wife, Madeline Catherine Smith, with much the same staffing levels as their predecessors. The couple also operated a horse-and-carriage hire service and livery stables from the premises. The stable building still remains on the south side of the car park and was converted a few years ago into residential accommodation. Following Henry's death in 1906, his widow continued running the hotel business and stables.

The Victoria Hotel remained a popular and successful venue for many decades and, in the Second World War, the garage attached to it was requisitioned by the Admiralty for use as a storage facility. The Assembly Room was demolished, many of the features of the garden disappeared, the accommodation of guests was discontinued and some of the land was sold off to form Olave Close. In the 1980s a small cache of Victorian 'Bun' Pennies was found during the demolition of some of the outbuildings to create the car park at the side of the main building. This provided the inspiration for the change of the name at that time to 'The Bun Penny'. Under this name the public house still flourishes and remains popular with locals and visitors alike.

Two Hotels That Never Were

When the proposed layout of the new resort was mapped out, apparently it was intended that the area bounded by what is now Pier Street on the east, Marine Parade West on the South, Milvil Road on the west and High Street on the north would be developed as a large hotel. On one of the first plans drawn up by the Lee-on-the-Solent Estates Company in 1884 the whole of this area is marked "Hotel Site". It was not until some seven years later that matters came to a head on this proposal. On Tuesday 29 September 1891 *The Portsmouth Evening News* reported:

Mr. E. Goble, on behalf of Sir Charles Robinson, applied for a provisional licence...for a new hotel proposed to be erected at Lee-on-the-Solent. He said that in 1883 the Lee estate was purchased by Sir Charles and in the following year a licence was granted for the Victoria Hotel there, which was still in existence, but was some distance from the beach. The estate had considerably progressed ... He need not say that an hotel placed in such a position would have considerable attractions to residents in our larger towns, who wished to use the seaside ... A syndicate had been formed for the erection of the proposed new hotel on land immediately opposite the pier. The hotel would be a large and commodious one ... He proceeded to put in and explain the plans of the proposed hotel, which was to have 42 bedrooms ... It would give an impetus to the surrounding properties, and would help the neighbouring farmers to get rid of their produce. No opposition whatever was raised to the application. Mr. A.F. Aldridge of Gracechurch Street, London, a member of the firm of solicitors to the Lee-on-the-Solent Hotel Syndicate, said he believed they were prepared to spend from £10,000 [£810,000] to £20,000 [£1,620,000] carrying out the works. Mr. C. Newton-Robinson ... stated ... the new hotel was very much required, the present one providing insufficient accommodation and possessing only five or six bedrooms ... Mr. C. Bovil Smith, surveyor, stated that within his experience two things were necessary to the success of a watering place – a church and a good hotel.

Clearly the proponents of the plan had put forward a strong case for the development of a new hotel, but the newspaper article continues:

The Magistrates having deliberated for a few minutes in private, the Chairman announced that they were unanimously of the opinion that one licensed house was sufficient for the requirements of the district. Without pledging themselves to anything, they might venture to tell the applicant that his only hope of getting a licence for a new hotel was to apply for a transfer of the licence from the existing one. The Magistrates had received a memorial on the subject from the Temperance League at Titchfield, and had given it their attention. Mr. Goble suggested whether the transfer of a licence from another part of the county to the new hotel might not be applied for. – The Chairman: No. We are unanimously of the opinion that one licensed house is amply sufficient for the neighbourhood.

With these few words the dreams and aspirations of the developers were shattered and we can only speculate how differently the story of Lee-on-the-Solent might have been had the magistrates approved the application.

On a plan of the estate from around the early 1890s there is another large area clearly marked "Hotel Site" on the north side of Grenville Road. Once again this venture never came to fruition, it being part of the large area of the westernmost portion of the town which was taken over by the Admiralty in 1917 as part of the naval air base.

Pier Hotel

We have already seen that one of the earliest buildings established in the new town in the 1880s was 'Trafalgar House' on the corner of Pier Street and Marine Parade East. As already mentioned in Chapter 9, the property was originally a private residence before being used as schools until 1907. By then the original building had been extended eastwards to provide considerable enlargement, and the extended section maintained the Dutch gable façade. In that year Frederick and Frances Hannen, who had moved from the Victoria Hotel and opened a restaurant in Pier Street in 1898, took over the premises and opened Hannen's House Hotel. They were assisted in the running of the business by their son, Joseph Frederick Charles Hannen who, together with his wife, Mable Grace Hannen, would later be the proprietor of the Inn by the Sea for many years.

Hannen's Private Hotel on the corner of Pier Street and Marine Parade East.
It later became Pier Hotel and later still Pier House

Later, when it was Pier Hotel, it was requisitioned by the Admiralty in 1939 as accommodation for WRNS. After the war, in 1949, when it had reverted to being a hotel, the proprietor, Capt Cutler, constructed a small landing stage known locally as 'Cutler's Pier' out of concrete blocks just opposite the hotel. From this, he ran trips into the Solent for hotel guests in his motorboat for a fee of 10s [£14.20] each. Shortly afterwards, in December 1950, he sold the premises and all the fixtures, furniture and equipment for £14,154 9s [£380,000] to Hampshire County Council which opened Pier House, a home for 31 elderly residents. It was one of ten such homes provided by Hampshire County Council at that time. This operated for many years before the building was completely demolished, apart from the Dutch gable façade, and redeveloped as private residential apartments in 2010.

Heylands Court Hotel

'Heylands' was situated on the corner of Beach Road and the High Street and dated from the first decade of the twentieth century. It was a large, rather grand-looking villa with a double frontage and comprised a ground, first and second floor. At the front of the building there was an attractive first-floor balcony lined with a neat wooden balustrade similar to those which can still be seen along the balconies of the first floor of the shops on the east side of Pier Street. The property was originally a private residence, one of the earliest occupants being a builder named Charles Wright who lived there with his wife, Florence.

Around the time of the end of the Great War it started to be used as a boarding house and an hotel under the name of 'Heylands Court Hotel'. The business flourished under a succession of various owners including Mrs Gibson, Miss Pike, Mrs Harrison and Mr and Mrs Woodger. During the Second World War it was requisitioned by the Admiralty for use as accommodation for WRNS, but opened again as a hotel following the end of hostilities.

In 1948, the Ministry of Works leased the building to provide accommodation for the local office of the Ministry of National Insurance. That office later closed and the property was used by the same Ministry as a staff-training centre. From June 1953, two rooms were occupied by the local food office. A flat was also maintained in the building for the principal of the staff-training centre.

Following closure, the building was left empty for some years and became rather dilapidated. It was finally demolished in the early 1980s and Hometide House retirement apartment block was built on the site.

Mansfield House Hotel

Being located on the corner of Milvil Road and Newton Place, this was the only hotel ever to be established on the western side of the town. Advertisements for it appeared each year on the cover of the local Kelly's Street Directories and showed that, in the 1930s, a week's full board was available for just three guineas [£175] and that the 'best English food' was provided.

In the Second World War, the Admiralty requisitioned the building so that it could be used for WRNS accommodation. Sadly, during a night-time bombing raid on HMS Daedalus on 23 November 1940, an anti-aircraft shell penetrated the roof of the building, exploded in the dining room and killed ten of the WRNS billeted there (see Chapter 19 and Appendix 4). After the War, the property returned to being an hotel for a brief period.

On 3 February 1922, an inaugural meeting of the Hampshire Association for the Care of the Blind was held with the purpose of taking over responsibility for the care of blind people, as laid on the County Council by The Blind Persons Act, 1920. The provision of a home for blind people was suggested in 1943 and the Association recommended that the County Council should establish such a home, providing the necessary care and attention while preserving the residents' individuality and independence in a way which was not possible in Public Assistance Institutions.

There is, in fact, quite a saga about how the home for the blind came into being. On 19 September 1952, *The Hampshire Telegraph and Post* reported that Gosport Borough Council had met to discuss a report by the Plans and Buildings Committee regarding the intention of Hampshire County Council to buy Mansfield House Hotel for use as a home for the blind. Prior to going into committee, Alderman H Turner said that the Planning Committee would not make any objection to the change of use, but he felt that the Council should know and register its opinion.

The following week Gosport Borough Council, in committee, registered a strong protest. The grounds for the objections were:-

1. The site was close to a Naval Air Operational Area and, with the increase of jet propulsion aircraft, the noise would be injurious to the nerves and therefore the health of the blind. (No, the authors did not make that up!)

2. A change of rate assessment for the building would produce a rate burden. No figures were quoted as to how much this would affect other rate-payers within the borough, possibly because it would be immeasurably small.

3. Two other institutions in the vicinity were already administered by Hampshire County Council. (Quite why this should have been a ground for objection is not entirely clear).

4. With one hotel (ie Pier Hotel) already taken over, the loss of a second would seriously reduce the amenities of the seaside town.

On 17 October it was reported that, because of local objections (a petition of 173 signatures had been received), the matter had been referred by the County Planning Committee to the Minister of Housing and Local Government for resolution.

In December, the local press reported that Gosport Borough Council had met and was divided over whether to continue with the opposition to the proposal; 27 members were in favour of continuing the objection but seven members were against doing so. In view of the petition signed by locals, the Council felt that it had no alternative other than to object to the proposal. However a councillor for Lee ward said that, after talking to local residents, he believed that 70 percent were in favour and 30 percent were against. Additionally, the Association for the Blind had something to say about the first objection and affirmed that blind people liked to listen to the sound of aircraft!

During early February 1953, Hampshire Planning Committee stated that the Minister of Housing had written to Gosport Borough Council saying that he did not think that there were sufficient grounds to require him to intervene formally. Most members of the County Planning Committee were of the opinion that consent should be given, but it was decided to defer the question for a month as a courtesy because Gosport Borough Council had not had a representative at the meeting. It was also understood that the Minister would be reviewing the whole position on a national basis within the following 18 months. Shortly afterwards, Gosport Borough Council reaffirmed its opposition to the plan and a deputation was appointed and a "lively debate" took place.

In April, Hampshire Planning Committee declared that the proposal was to proceed because it had been approved by the Minister of Housing and Local Government. Gosport Borough Council then suggested another property be used, but it was overruled as Mansfield House Hotel, with its large number of small bedrooms, was ideally suited for the purpose for which it was required. Any house with large rooms would be costly to adapt and would be unsuitable for other reasons. Thus the blind home was finally established.

In August 1954 it was the scene of great excitement when a blind couple, Jack and Sue Cumming, who had married at Christchurch, travelled to the home for their honeymoon. They were welcomed by the residents, who formed a guard of honour at the main entrance and made an archway with their white sticks. The couple entered the building to the strains of the Wedding March. A bridal suite had already been established for the newly married couple.

In the October of 1954, more than two years after it was first mooted, Mansfield House was officially opened by the Mayor of Gosport, Alderman A J Eales. The first residents had moved in on 26 June and, by October, there were 25 blind and partially sighted residents. The Mayor said the home had an important part to play in local life and in forming local traditions. It would eventually accommodate 31 people. Alderman Osborn said the success of the home depended mainly on the people of Lee-on-the-Solent and Gosport: "If we say we will in every way help these people who are living at Mansfield House, I am certain our labours will be well rewarded".

The final seal of approval came at the beginning of February 1955 when Dr Reginald Bennett, the local MP, visited the home. He was shown round by Mr Back, the Warden, and he spoke to many of the residents. Mr Back later said that Dr Bennett had been very impressed with the smooth-running of the establishment.

The home continued to cater for the blind for many years before becoming a nursing home for the elderly. The building is now the Glen Heathers Nursing Home, which is part of Saffronland Homes, and caters for about 53 residents.

The Belle Vue Hotel

One of the earliest villas to be established in the building plots along Marine Parade East in the late 1880s was 'Belle Vue'. Built as a private residence for Mr W Perrin, it was later let out and changed ownership a number of times before opening as an hotel in the 1920s. It soon acquired two such neighbouring villas and, once again, became a popular and successful establishment. In the 1940s the proprietors were Charles George Webb and his wife who, in their advertisements, gave the public *A few reasons why you should stay at the Belle Vue Hotel*. These included:

Unrivalled cuisine

Comfortable beds, all rooms exceptionally well furnished

Hot and cold water, gas and electric fires in all bedrooms. Central heating

The only hotel commanding an uninterrupted view of the Isle of Wight and shipping entering the Solent

Sun Parlour

Private lock-up garages

Infra-red Ray Treatment available

Five minutes from 18-hole golf course.

Over the years the hotel expanded until it was able to boast 27 bedrooms and an AA 3-star rating. For many years it was the only hotel operating in the town and towards the end of its life the 'Seasons' restaurant and the visiting entertainment was enjoyed by many. In 2002, owners Tony Bellasis and Peter Driscoll's plans for further expansion were halted by local objections and they decided to sell the site. The business closed its doors for the last time on 31 March 2003, the building was soon demolished and the site redeveloped by the construction of the Anchorage Court retirement apartments. With the passing of the business, Lee-on-the-Solent lost its long-standing ability to offer hotel accommodation to both visitors and locals alike.

12.

SPLASHING OUT

When, in 1931, it was announced that work was about to begin on the construction of a swimming pool at the western end of Lee-on-the-Solent, various people in the town became a little uncomfortable. They expressed their concerns that the coast defences should be improved at that spot before any excavations for the swimming pool were initiated, but they were ignored and the digging commenced. This proved to be a classic case of a little local knowledge being a valuable thing. When the cliffs at the site had been excavated to below the level of the beach, a particularly high tide combined with a strong onshore wind caused the site become completely flooded with seawater. One can imagine the "We told you so!" reaction from the locals. The contractors learnt their lesson.

When the swimming pool was complete it became Britain's first and only heated outdoor seawater bathing-pool. At 240 ft *[73m]* in length it was considerably longer than modern Olympic-sized pools which are only 164 ft long *[50m]*. It was 40 ft *[12m]* wide with a springboard and two fixed boards about 8 ft *[2.5m]* and 16 ft *[5m]* high at the deep, eastern end. When swimming galas and water-polo matches were held they drew large crowds, particularly as spectators could watch from the surrounding cliff-tops. However, it was not possible to observe the activities from the side adjacent to the sea, as there were wooden changing cubicles on the seaward side of the pool, there being no promenade at that time and the beach being much lower.

Although the pool was still available for general public use during the Second World War, it was the subject of a requisitioning order by

A swimming gala at the swimming pool, 1932

the Admiralty to enable military personnel to use it at certain times for swimming instruction and practice.

On 5 July 1945 there was a Service Aquatics event at the pool at which six Service Establishments competed. Earlier that summer, on some evenings, it was possible to see some local young lads (one of the authors being among their number) being taught how to dive from the diving boards by a German prisoner of war, who often stopped off for a swim as he walked back from work in Bridgemary to be locked up for the night in Stubbington. There were large numbers of German prisoners of war involved in the building of Bridgemary.

Unfortunately it was not long before the pool, like many of the other public facilities in Lee, began to run into financial difficulties. In May 1949 a plan was announced to convert it into a children's paddling pool at a cost of £2,700 *[£78,300]*. It was the view of local councillors that this was the most economic way of dealing with the facility, which was already costing ratepayers £1,000 *[£29,000]* a year to maintain. Attendance at the pool barely warranted the cost of employing the staff required to keep it open. Additionally, the Ministry of Health regulations stipulated that, if the facility was to be maintained as a public swimming pool, a new water filtration plant, costing £6,000 *[£174,000]*, would need to be installed. Work was therefore undertaken to convert the site into two paddling pools. One of these was for toddlers and had a depth of 6 inches *[15cm]* and the other, for small children, had a depth ranging from 1 ft 3 ins *[37cm]* to 2 ft 3 ins*[67cm]*. As part of this building programme, a new path was provided to enable prams and pushchairs to be wheeled down from the cliff-top to the site. Additionally, the changing cubicles at the swimming pool were dismantled and the timber from them was recycled and used to construct beach huts to the west of Lee Tower. Those huts were then rented out and the revenue received was used to cover some of the cost of the conversion works at the pool. Some years later, the whole pool was completely filled in to make a playground area.

13

A MONUMENT FOR ALL TIME

In 1934, two years after the pier caught fire, foundation work began on the construction of a then state-of-the-art pleasure feature on the seafront – the Art Deco style Lee Tower complex.

Viewed from the air, the building – together with the remains of the pier – formed a Y shape, with the top part of the Y enclosing a semicircular remembrance garden. On the ground floor of the west arm of the Y was a 'winter garden' – a hall with a sprung floor which was mainly used as a ballroom but also hosted a variety of civic and private functions. Next to this was a concourse, buffet bar and service kitchens. On the first floor above the ballroom was the Palm Court Café and restaurant. The east arm of the Y consisted of a first-rate little cinema with stalls and a circle, with a short stairway on either side. It had a seating capacity of 950.

Construction work was quite laborious. The workmen used picks and spades – without any mechanical diggers – and all the bricks used in the construction of the Tower were made in the brick kilns at Lee. At the centre of the complex was a 120ft *[36m]* high tower with a lift and stairs to a viewing platform at the top where outstanding views of the Solent could be enjoyed. When complete, the whole structure was rendered and finished in crisp clean white – adding to its attractive appearance.

At the time that the railway at Lee was closing down, Lee Tower was nearing completion, and it is reasonable to assume that some of the last freight transported would have been material used in the Tower's construction. Three months after the closing of the railway, the opening ceremony for Lee Tower was held at 6pm on 26 December 1935. It was conducted by Admiral Sir Arthur Waistell, who was assisted by the Mayor. A Universal News presentation, a cartoon and two films were shown in the cinema that evening.

A Souvenir Programme given out at the opening ceremony set out a brief description of the Tower complex and the facilities which were available to be enjoyed there. It said that:

The Cinema forms part of one of the most magnificent and imposing edifices in the South of England, which in the near future will be known throughout the Country.

Its origin is entirely due to the enterprise and courage displayed by the Chairman of Solent Properties Ltd., Colonel J. Williams C.B.E. who seeing the outstanding position of Lee-on-the-Solent as a modern Seaside resort, determined to build such a structure that any king would be pleased to claim as theirs.

The Architecture and Designing was entrusted to one of the most eminent firms of architects in the country, namely, Messrs. Yates, Cook & Darbyshire, of 43 Great Marlborough Street, London, who are to be congratulated upon the majestic and stately lines of the Building.

The whole structure comprising the Cinema, Dance Hall, Restaurant, Lounge, and Saloon Bars, with a perfect Roof Terrace, and rising above it all, the Lee Tower itself, fitted with a luxury passenger lift to convey patrons to the 120 ft. [36m] high platform, which gives an unrivalled sea view of the Solent and Channel. It has been erected by one of our best-known Builders and Townsmen, Mr. A. Prestidge, of Lee-on-the-Solent, and it need hardly be added, that it will remain as a Monument of craftsmanship and energy to him for all time.

The builder, Mr Arthur Prestidge, was also one of the directors of Solent Properties Ltd.

Nikolaus Pevsner, the renowned architectural historian, said of the design that it reminded him of an elongated cigarette lighter. He thought it "jazzy" with "a rather nice elegant vulgarity."

For children, on Saturday mornings, a cinema entrance ticket to the stalls in the Tower complex, during and just after war, cost 3d

[43p], and for the circle it was 6d [86p]. For that princely sum there would be two films, one or two cartoons and perhaps a Pathé News. It was not unknown for youngsters to pay to go downstairs and then sneak up one of the stairways, most times being caught by an usherette, and either sent back down or ejected from the cinema. The prices were significantly dearer in the evenings; 1s [£1.75] for the stalls and 1s 9d [£3] for the circle. The films were changed every Monday, Thursday, and Sunday giving six different films plus the Saturday morning matinee, and the Pearl & Deane trailers and advertisements.

The Art Deco complex was the jewel in the crown of Lee-on-the-Solent and, with its brilliant white appearance, it made a lasting impression on all who saw it. During the Second World War the whole complex was painted in camouflage colours but restored to its white mantle after the War.

Looking west along the beach to the Tower and the Pier

In the 1940s, 1950s and 1960s, Lee Tower was the absolute focus of life in Lee-on-the-Solent. When making arrangements the most frequently heard phrase was "See you up the Tower" meaning the entrance to the ballroom or cinema.

The ballroom on the west side of the Tower was also used as a gymnasium by the Fleet Air Arm. In the 1950s the resident band was the Bert Sharpe Band, although there had been a number of other bands who played there on different occasions. A news notice of December 1950 announced: *Public dances at Lee Tower Mondays, Wednesdays and Saturdays, not Christmas Day* and, in June 1954: *A clock was installed on Lee Tower.*

Between the Tower and Marine Parade was the remembrance garden, with the war memorial in the centre. The gardens were in the shape of a semicircle and the buses to Gosport and Fareham would pull into the semicircular road and stop in front of the Tower in what was a one-way system. Advertisements for the cinema stated that: *All buses stop at the covered entrance to the Vestibule.*

As a safety measure, the Tower complex was closed briefly in early July 1940 so that works to breach the pier could be undertaken. Orders were also issued that the foreshore at Stokes Bay and Lee south of the road were to be closed entirely to the general public. Bathing huts were removed and kiosks closed. Once the breaching of the pier had been completed, all the facilities reopened.

As mentioned in Chapter 5, it was decided that Lee-on-the-Solent would be the base for CO-TUG (the Anglo-American tug unit responsible for organising the transport of Mulberry Harbour components to Normandy) as part of the preparations for D-Day in 1944. This unit had its headquarters in Lee Tower before moving to London on 18 December 1944.

Sadly, on May 24 1945, there was a tragic accident at the Tower. It was reported in the press as: *Lee Girl killed by a fall of concrete at the Ballroom at Lee Tower. Her death was a result of haemorrhage due to injuries accidentally received when struck by a piece of concrete falling from a building was the verdict on Renee Jones of 3 Petrie Road, Lee-on-the-Solent. She was standing talking to a sailor outside the ballroom of Lee Tower — cracked concrete may have been caused by earlier nearby bombing or the blowing up of the pier.*

The Tower complex from the landward side

The Tower remained the heart of Lee-on-the-Solent for 36 years, but unfortunately the sentiments expressed at its opening proclaiming that it would be a monument for all time proved to be somewhat over optimistic. In 1937 the company which ran the Tower went into liquidation and leases of various parts of the complex were granted to interested parties. The facility was losing money over a long period, possibly due to problems with overall management, and various attempts to diversify and promote the businesses failed to improve its fortunes. The cinema stopped showing films in 1961 and was put to various uses thereafter, including an unsuccessful term as a ten-pin bowling venue. Eventually Gosport Borough Council, as ultimate owner of the complex, decided that it had to go and, after much discussion concerning alternative uses for the site, the whole building was demolished in the spring of 1971.

14

BESIDE THE SEASIDE BESIDE THE SEA

The original sea wall was constructed by the Lee-on-the-Solent Railway Company in 1894, alongside the railway terminus, and extended for about a quarter of a mile towards Elmore. This was one of the very first coastal defences and reinforcements to appear in the area and would be just the start of a programme of works which still continues to this day. In December 1899 *The Hampshire Telegraph* carried an official notice reciting an application made by Sir John Charles Robinson for *permission to construct a series of 66 groynes upon the foreshore between Stubbington lane and the eastern end of Marine Parade East, Lee-on-the-Solent.*

In the 1920s the beach featured in the news again, but for tragic reasons. On 27 September 1927, Miss Winifred Spears (21) of Albert Road, Gosport, left home to attend a meeting of the Girl Guides but she never reached her destination. Despite an active search, no trace of her was found until her body was discovered washed up on the foreshore at Lee-on-the-Solent. While she had left home in good spirits and in good health, it was revealed that she had suffered a nervous breakdown earlier that year. An inquest returned a verdict of "suicide while of unsound mind". A year later, the naked body of Mr A W Harley, who was the Town Clerk of Christchurch near Bournemouth, was washed ashore at Lee on 22 June. His clothes had been found at Mudeford earlier that week. An inquest held at Fareham heard evidence from the deceased's son-in-law stating that Harley's daughter had been involved in a serious motor accident shortly before. Some proceedings for damages were pending in that connection and Harley had shown signs of considerable worry about this. The witness went on to say that he did not think that the deceased was physically able to carry on his work as Town Clerk and Borough Accountant. The Coroner expressed his opinion that, owing to the worry of his work and the motor accident, Harley was not responsible for his actions and a verdict of "suicide whilst temporarily insane" was returned.

Despite its relatively sheltered position, the resort's coastline has been the focus of a number of problems arising from adverse weather. In the winter of 1946-7 a small coaster was driven on to the beach near the sailing club, where it remained for a few days until it was pulled off by tugs. The Cunard liner *Queen Elizabeth* went aground on the Brambles Sandbank near the end of Southampton Water in April 1947 and in August 1949 a news report recorded that: *Choppy seas after mid-day played havoc with the hydroplane racing at Lee, there were 3,000 spectators, also at the event was a replica Viking ship* (as on the crest of the Borough of Gosport).

In June 1949, Gosport Borough Council approved a proposal costing £14,000 *[£406,000]* for development of the cliffs at Lee "from their rough and virgin condition". This included the provision of parking for 300 cars (£2,500) *[£72,500]*, the construction of sunken rock gardens (£3,000) *[£87,000]*, the laying of lawns and flower-beds (£1,500) *[£43,500]* and the building of two new public conveniences (£7,000) *[£203,000]*. Nevertheless, in October of that year, it was announced that the cost was considered prohibitive and the whole scheme was abandoned.

When five days of atrocious gales, including wind speeds of up to 40 knots, resulted in a 100 ft *[30m]* frontage of the cliff being washed away early in December 1954, it was realised that a more extensive sea wall was needed. This incident represented just one more case in a long line of problems concerning coastal defence at Lee. Indeed, between 1909 and 1953, successive storms had eroded the cliff face by between 20 ft *[6m]* and 60 ft *[18m]* along the entire frontage. In January 1955 it was decided that urgent work needed to be undertaken immediately in order to prevent the complete loss of the clifflands and their amenities. The proposals included the installation of steel

From the Tower looking east and showing the limited extent of the promenade, 1950s

piling with concrete capping and the cliff being graded off to an angle of 45 degrees, a paved promenade with lighting, a dwarf wall with steps to the beach, and an extension of the sea wall both to the east and to the west. At the same time, the existing wooden groynes were to be improved and others constructed. The promenade was also to be widened and a deckchair area, some 50 ft *[15m]* wide, provided. Of course, all of this came at a cost – some £67,000 *[£1,370,000]* in fact. This sum was borrowed on loan, repayable over 20 years, and represented a 2½d *[22p]* increase in the rate assessment.

In October of that year, the Lee coastal defence scheme was still a 'hot potato' on the local political front. It was generally accepted that a scheme to prevent further erosion was needed as quickly as possible and several schemes were discussed, one of which would have cost as much as £250,000 *[£5,120,000]*. While the cost of the chosen scheme was quoted at £67,000 *[£1,370,000]*, due to an increase in labour costs the price quickly rose to £73,000 *[£1,490,000]* and it was likely to go even higher. Those members of the Council who were successful in getting this more modest scheme adopted were both quick and emphatic to point out that there would be no part in it for the construction of any bandstands, swimming pools or towers on the foreshore. In short, only the minimum necessary would be carried out. The Borough Engineer said that the cliffs would now be sloped to a 20 ft *[6m]* promenade, but no shelters or electric lights would be erected due to the heavy and escalating costs. It was all yet another nail in the coffin of Sir John Robinson's dream of creating a premier seaside resort.

The work was completed in the early 1960s. Unfortunately, the extension of the promenade covered an internationally important geological Site of Special Scientific Interest. Prior to that time, evidence of rare and previously unrecorded fauna, including 13 unique scientific species, had been discovered in the Bracklesham Beds layer at Lee-on-the-Solent.

The great storm of October 1987 and the January storms of 1990 caused substantial beach erosion. It was apparent that the beach shingle was becoming significantly depleted and that further action was needed to protect the coastline.

In 1992 there was a complete failure of part of the sea wall about 220 yards *[200m]* from the old railway terminus. This failure may have been caused in part by previous damage caused by a bomb that fell during the Second World War in that area on the promenade.

Between September 1996 and March 1997 11 rock groynes were constructed and the beach was built up using aggregates dredged from Southampton Water. Dredgers pumped the aggregates on to the beach at Elmore, where it was moved by diggers and trucks on to the cliffs near the angling club to form a huge mound. The trucks were then used to move, deposit and spread the material along the whole length of the beach between Hill Head and Elmore, covering some parts up to six feet *[1.8m]* in depth. The whole operation took four months to complete.

After the Second World War, a favourite swimming area for most youngsters from Elmore was near the sailing club. Here, in the shingle on the beach, it was quite common to find the fossilised sharks' teeth mentioned in Chapter 1. There was also an island that appeared just before low tide which was known as 'cockle island', although it actually consisted mainly of mussel shells. In the summer, yachts were tied up to buoys near the island but sometimes, if the weather turned bad, they were brought ashore. Mr Joseph Frederick Charles Hannen was the commodore of the sailing club and his yacht was called *Timtura*, the same name as his house on the corner of Cambridge Road. As mentioned in Chapter 11, he was son of Frederick Hannen, who opened the Victoria Inn in 1884, and was also the landlord of the Inn-by-the-Sea.

15

CLIFFS AND BUTTS

The coastline from Titchfield Haven to Browndown formerly consisted of cliffs with a height of about 23 ft *[7m]* in some places reducing to just over 4 ft *[1.2m]* in other areas such as Elmore. At the base of the cliffs was a shingle beach which, at high tide, was on average about 16 ft *[5m]* wide. At Lee-on-the-Solent the cliffs have now been replaced by sloping banks, but were on average about 16 ft *[5m]* high. They continued eastward, reducing to 3 ft *[less than 1m]* in height near Elmore Lake before gradually increasing again to about 16 ft *[5m]*. After about 350 yards *[320m]* eastwards from the Elmore Lake area, the line of the cliffs curves sharply inland at about 45 degrees before taking a more gentle angle to meet the river Alver. This mile long stretch has been the subject of longshore drift which, in the distant past, resulted in a maximum 500 yard *[450m]*-wide area of flat scrubland, composed of shingle and sediment, upon which gorse and heather became established. This area comprises about 156 acres, is quite unsuitable for farming, and is what we know today as Browndown.

Children on the beach near The Old Ship Public House in 1958. Note how high the cliffs were at that time

A map of 948 shows it as 'Brun Down', and in 1277 the Manor of Rowner was granted by King Edward I to Sir William le Brun, whose descendants have been closely associated with Gosport and Rowner right up to recent times. Over the years the name evolved to become 'Brune' and is now seen in 'Brune Park'.

On a map of 1587 the area to the west of 'Gamoore pond' (Gomer Pond) is shown as 'Browne Down'. The name becomes 'Bare down' on a map of 1759 but evolves into 'Brown down' on a later map produced in 1791 (see Appendix 6). Some 16 acres were in Alverstoke Parish and 140 acres were in Titchfield parish and formed the eastern end of the Titchfield Abbey estates. It has already been seen how these estates became the property of the Wriothesleys, Earls of Southampton, after the Dissolution. In 1741 these estates, including Browndown, were sold to Peter Delmé.

In the second half of the eighteenth century, a programme to build various local defensive structures was initiated in the area. At the start of the American War of Independence in 1779, work began on the building of Fort Monckton at the eastern end of Stokes Bay to help protect Portsmouth Harbour. The Governor of Portsmouth, Lt General Sir Robert Monckton, instructed his Commanding Engineer, Lt Col John Archer, to draw up plans for the defence of Stokes Bay. In 1779, a new temporary fort was constructed at Gilkicker Point consisting of a 6 ft *[1.8m]*-thick earth bank supported by brushwood fascines. The structure was so inadequate that the tents of the soldiers billeted in the fort were blown away in 1780. Archer proposed a new permanent structure, which was accepted in July 1780. It was to be called 'The Fort at Gilkicker' and construction started in September 1780 but, as a consequence of using a mixture of civilian and conscripted labour, work proceeded at a very slow pace. The design was criticised by Charles Lennox, 3rd Duke of Richmond, who in 1782, was appointed as Master-General of the Ordnance. As a consequence, Archer was removed from his post in 1783 and the construction was taken over by an engineer officer, James Glenie, who in turn was removed in 1784. This resulted once again in a slowing down of the building work: more controversy ensued regarding the design and the name of the fort. It was renamed Fort Monckton, after Sir Robert Monkton, who died in 1782. The fort was not completed until 1793 and was rebuilt in the 1880s as part of Lord Palmerston's ring of defensive forts around Portsmouth.

In 1782 the Board of Ordnance (the precursor of the Ministry of Defence) ordered plans to be drawn up for the fortification of Stokes Bay and these included defences to be built on Browndown. Nothing happened until 1783-1784, when the Board bought the whole coast from Portsmouth Harbour westwards. At the eastern end of Browndown, 25 acres were bought from the Delmé family, and over the next 50 years or so, up to 1838, the government's holding at Browndown increased to 30 acres.

Between 1784 and 1838, the site at Browndown was in all probability used for musketry practice. If, as Lesley Burton wrote in 'Browndown Musketry and Mutineers', the first butts (ie backstops for the musket balls) on the musketry range at Browndown were constructed by French prisoners in about 1804, it would mean that those butts would have been to the east of the present-day track leading to Browndown Battery (built 1852). The prisoners who built these butts were marched from Forton Prison and guarded by Royal Marines from Clarence Barracks in Portsmouth. Other features such as mantlets (a medieval word for a shield or shelter used for stopping arrows or bullets) were probably also built around this time.

In the 1940s, the remains of a derelict butt were still to be found just inside perimeter fence at the western end of the rifle range. This suggests that this would have been the first butt built after the government took possession of the western end of Browndown, 100 years earlier in 1840. Maps of the area give a good indication as to where the material for this butt, and others later, was obtained. A hundred yards [90m] into the deposition site of the longshore drift on the western end, the cliff has been excavated for a width and depth of over 60 ft [18.2m] (see Appendix 6). Over 50 years later, between 1893 and 1898, when the longer-distance ranges were constructed, it seems very likely that the material for these new butts would have been taken from this 'cutting' into the cliff, especially as the narrow-gauge railway was constructed at the same time and the railway tracks went to the locations of these butts.

Also during the 1940s, each butt was identified by a large wooden letter, about six ft *[1.8m]* high, firmly fixed on the top and in the middle of each butt facing along the line of fire. The letters were clearly visible from the top decks of buses travelling along Portsmouth Road. On each side of the letter, and equally spaced along the ridge of the butts, there were numbers 1 to 5 on one side and 6 to 10 on the other for each target position. The butts were A, B, C and D, with A being the most westerly. The butt identity markers had been there for some time and may even have been there when the butts were originally built, possibly in the 1890s.

In what might now be termed 'a classic government U-turn', the Board of Ordnance decided to sell off most of the western part of its Stokes Bay land in 1839 and the 25 acres it had earlier bought at Browndown returned to the ownership of the Delmé family. Selling back this land was an unfortunate decision because by 1851, when it was perceived that there was a possibility of a French attack or invasion, an urgent programme of building new fortifications had to be embarked upon. The government was then forced to buy back much of the land it had sold between 1839 and 1840. This time, however, it bought the complete 156 acres of Browndown including 125 acres from the Delmé family, 13 acres from John Leveson Gower, and 17 acres from David Compigne.

Browndown is the site of the last recorded fatal duel between two Englishmen. The duel took place at sunset on 20 May 1845 between Lt Henry Hawkey of the Royal Marines and Capt James Seton late of the 11th Dragoons. Seton had apparently paid too much attention to Hawkey's wife and called on her whenever her husband was absent with his duties. Although both parties lived in Portsmouth, they chose Browndown as the venue for their duel because it was quite secluded and they were less likely to be interrupted.

The duel started as a bit of fiasco and the first attempt was a failure – Hawkey's pistol failed to fire, while Seton missed completely. Their standard of proficiency may well bring to mind the words attributed to the Duke of Wellington: "I don't know what effect these men will have on the enemy but, by God, they terrify me!" Usually, in these circumstances the parties would consider the matter settled and, with 'honour' duly satisfied, they would retire. In this case, Hawkey demanded a second attempt in which Seton missed again but was hit by Hawkey's bullet. He was taken from Browndown beach to a yacht and then to Portsmouth where he died nearly two weeks later on 2 June.

Hawkey and his second, Lt Pym, stood trial at Winchester in March 1846, where their lawyer successfully claimed that Seton's death was a result of the intrusive and incompetent medical treatment that he had received following the duel: Hawkey and Pym were both found not guilty.

Two earthwork batteries were constructed at Browndown Point at the east end of the Browndown site by 1852. *The Hampshire Telegraph* reported on 6 September 1851 that a company of sappers was sent from Fort Monckton barracks to assist in the construction of these batteries. They were not in use for very long, were heavily criticised for their inadequacy, and the eastern one was demolished by 1860. The western one was replaced by a more substantial battery, Browndown Battery, in 1888.

In 1856 a camp was established to accommodate The Anglo-German Legion, which was a group of German soldiers recruited to fight for Britain in the Crimean War. The armistice had occurred in the Crimea on 29 February of that year and these soldiers had just returned from Scutari. On July 25 1856 *The Morning Post* reported:

During the past few days a new camp has been formed at a place called Browndown, a well situated piece of ground for such a purpose, about four miles from this garrison, on the Gosport side of the harbour, and on the banks of the Solent, almost immediately opposite Osborne House. The camp has, in the first place, been taken up by about 1,300 men of the British Foreign Legion, who have just come home from Scutari.

They are expected to be joined shortly by other regiments, and, amongst others, by those who have been for a fortnight or so at Aldershot.

About 6,000 men are, it is understood, to be quartered at this camp; but whether permanently or not is not known.

The locality of the camp is a slightly elevated strip of land, exceedingly dry and apparently very salubriously situated. Water of a good quality seems to be very abundant; a number of wells having been sunk for the supply of whatever troops might be located here. The whole of the men are under canvas, the ordinary military tent being employed. There are about 130 tents in all, 10 or 12 men being accommodated in each; but to the officers a large proportionate number is allotted. Colonel Dickenson, commandant of the Swiss Legion is senior officer. A fine view of the camp, with its white tents, is to be obtained from her Majesty's marine residence at Osborne, which is clearly discernible from the camp ground. A canteen for the sale of beer, spirits, and tobacco has already been established, and numerous provision dealers have commenced pursuing their avocations among the troops.

On 3 August 1856, 900 officers and men arrived at the camp, followed by a further 1,600 men on the 4 August. Nine days later it was reported that the 1st and 3rd Regiments of Light Infantry were also encamped at Browndown.

The area was then honoured by a royal visit on 23 August 1856. Her Majesty Queen Victoria, Prince Albert, and the Prince of Wales landed at Stokes Bay (a pier had been built there in 1842 for the convenience of Queen Victoria when she visited the Isle of Wight) and from there they went on to visit the encampment. In her diary the Queen wrote:

... steamed in the Fairy across to Angleseaville, where we landed being received by Maj-Gen. Breton and his staff, a detachment of the 22nd forming a Guard of Honour. Entered carriage (the 2 boys driving with us) and drove a short way out to Browndown, a fine healthy campment only a few 100 yards from the sea where the 1st Brigade of the German Legions under the command of Brig. Gen. Wooldridge was drawn up. We drove down the line. Wooldridge himself is an intelligent man, has served with English troops, but was before *in the Spanish and Portuguese service.We drove to look at Gomer Fort which is in process of construction and then embarked getting home by ½ past 7.*

This is how one newspaper reported the event:

On Saturday last her Majesty and H.R.H. Prince Albert, accompanied by the Prince of Wales, the Princess Royal, and a few more of the Royal family, crossed from Osborne to Browndown, to review the troops of the British Foreign Legion, encamped there. Her Majesty arrived at the beach at Browndown at about half-past four o'clock, and was received by the Lieutenant-Governor, Major-General Breton, Commandant of the Camp Colonel Wooldridge, by a number of the officers of the Staff and Garrison, and a guard of honour from the 22ⁿᵈ Regiment, with its band. Two of the Royal carriages were in waiting for Her Majesty's use, in one of which Her Majesty and Prince Albert took their seats, and in the other H.R.H. the Princess Royal took hers. Her Majesty and H.R.H. Prince Albert were in private clothes. The road from the beach to the camp, about three quarters of a mile in length, was guarded by the 22ⁿᵈ Regiment and a detachment of the Legion.The troops to be reviewed were drawn up on the Down in line, two deep, and presented a fine soldierly appearance.They consisted of the 1ˢᵗ and 3ʳᵈ Regiments of the British German Legion, numbering about 2,000 men. Her Majesty drove in front of the line, accompanied by the officers in attendance, the band of each regiment playing appropriate tunes.

Afterwards the troops formed an open column, and marched past the Queen in quick and slow time, and no body of troops could have presented a finer appearance. Some other evolutions took place, after which Her Majesty and the Court went over the camp, the troops being drawn up in companies in front of their respective encampments; Her Majesty and suite walking round the whole of the camp, and entering some of the tents to view their accommodation, &c.

This being concluded, the Queen, the Prince, and the Court drove to the new forts, constructing near Browndown, and made a lengthened inspection of them.The royal party then returned to the beach, and re-embarked on board the Fairy, at half-past six in the evening, under a salute from the ships at Spithead.

The Times also reported on this event and added that: *Browndown is a capital spot for a permanent military settlement; 5,000 troops can be comfortably and most healthily camped there; the water is good and abundant; it is easy of access by sea and road; and no sooner does rain cease than the ground is perfectly dry.*

Within three months of their arrival, it appears that the Anglo-German Legion had outstayed its welcome with the local inhabitants. By November 1856 it had earned a reputation as being riotous and the civilians at Browndown were unhappy, as they felt that the Germans had been allowed to invade their usually serene locality. Arrangements were made for the departure of the Legion at the earliest opportunity and the soldiers embarked on a troop ship in November 1856 at Portsmouth Dockyard without any more incidents. It may seem a little bewildering as to whom the local inhabitants were, and why the proposed plan to have a permanent camp was so quickly dismissed. Perhaps the answer lies in the following.

Close to Alverstoke and a little nearer to the shore was Anglesey or Angleseyville. In *The Story of Gosport* by L F White he writes the following: *This beautiful village of modern date commands extensive views of the Isle of Wight, Spithead, and the Motherbank, the first stone having been laid by the Marquis of Anglesey in the year 1826. A chapel of ease was opened in 1844, dedicated to St. Mark. Here is a large hotel, reading rooms, baths and public gardens. The situation is very elevated and the surrounding scenery so commands universal admiration for its beauty and great variety, and in summer months, is much frequented by gentry for the benefit of its sea bathing and the beauties of its scenery.* No traders lived at Anglesey, only gentry, and these resided in The Crescent or in St Mark's Place.

Thus the troops were despatched, despite the already mentioned comment in *The Times* regarding the advantages of Browndown for troop encampment and the fact that this was a frantic time for building up the defences of the realm.

Although Browndown camp became unoccupied, the rifle range continued to be used for firing practice by the regular troops billeted at Fort Gomer. It was no doubt later used by those stationed at other forts as they were built – Fort Rowner in 1858, Fort Grange and Fort Brockhurst in 1858-1863, and possibly Fort Elson which had been built in 1855. Additionally a new barracks was built in Clarence Road, Gosport, capable of accommodating 1,000 troops with their officers, and it would seem most likely that they also would have used Browndown ranges. Volunteer troops also used the range for annual training. The Gosport Volunteers used the range for their annual rifle competition in 1868, firing Snider Enfield rifles as immortalised in Rudyard Kipling's poem, *The Grave of the Hundred Head*:

> *A Snider squibbed in the jungle -*
> *Somebody laughed and fled,*
> *And the men of the first Shikaris*
> *Picked up their Subaltern dead,*
> *With a big blue mark in his forehead*
> *And the back blown out of his head.*

In 1870 the new Martini-Henry rifle was tested at Browndown ranges. *The Times* of 26 January 1870 reported that: *...the Martini-Henry rifles...are now being subjected to a series of practical tests over the army rifle ranges on Browndown near Gosport. So far, the opinion appears to be that the new weapon is very superior to the Snider, but that many of the details connected both with the weapon itself and its equipment are open to considerable improvement.*

The Martini-Henry rifle was released in June 1871. It was faster-loading and had a longer range than the Snider that it replaced. Although it was no longer produced after 1889, it was still in service until the end of the Great War. A testament to its effectiveness lies in the fact that, as recently as 2010 and 2011, US marines recovered at least three of these rifles from various Taliban weapon caches in Marjah in the Helmand province of Afghanistan.

On 26 June 1870 *The Times* carried the following item:

A fatal accident occurred at the rifle ranges at Browndown near Gosport on Wednesday. A party belonging to the 64th Regiment was practising at the butts. While Private Edwards was in the act of taking aim, the marker, a private soldier named MacCabe, without waiting for the bugle call to cease firing, came from behind to whitewash the target and was shot dead.

Another fatality at the camp occurred in June 1894. Private Hendon was at work on the lawn outside the officers' quarters when he heard a single gunshot coming from inside. He rushed in and found Lt Walter Wallis Gill of the Royal Marines on his bed, bleeding profusely from a bullet wound to the abdomen. A recently discharged Martini-Henry rifle was lying on the floor. Gill, who had been at Browndown undergoing a course of musketry instruction, was given immediate medical attention but died shortly afterwards. Reports do not conclude whether his death was a result of an accident or suicide.

Another widely reported incident occurred early on Christmas Day, 1898. James Whatmore, a Private in the Royal Marine Light Infantry and Private Henry Spurrier of the same corps, were in a hut at Browndown with others on that morning when an alarm was raised that Whatmore had been stabbed by Spurrier. When asked why he had done it Spurrier replied "I only meant to just prick him to buck him up". Spurrier was sober and no angry words had passed between him and Whatmore, although the assailant had been depressed for some time, as if he had something on his mind. Whatmore, who had suffered a wound to the heart, died almost immediately and was later buried at Haslar. When he was arrested, Spurrier did not appear to understand what had happened. At his trial at Winchester Assizes on 13 February 1899, evidence showed that Spurrier had a history of epilepsy and that he had killed Whatmore while in a dazed state shortly after a seizure. Medical evidence also showed that Spurrier was probably unable to understand what he was doing. The prisoner was found guilty but insane and sentenced to be detained at Her Majesty's pleasure.

On 11 October 1883, manoeuvres were carried out to represent a mock attack in which a hostile force, intent on attacking Gosport, had landed at Browndown. This exercise involved all of the troops of the garrison at Portsmouth in much "skirmishing and manoeuvring". A similar sort of exercise would be undertaken 130 years later (see below).

In 1887 a news item reported that 7,000 regular troops used the range for individual firing, plus 2,500 for field practice in addition to

3,000 at the annual competition meetings.

The following was recorded in *Hansard*:

18th July 1888 War Office – the Solent – new bye-laws

Sir Frederick Fitz-Wygram *(Hants, Fareham) asked the President of the Board of Trade whether his attention had been called to the fact that if the bye-laws proposed by the Secretary of State for War for the prevention of vessels anchoring or sailing over the waters of the Solent off the rifle ranges at Brown down (within 1,600 yards [1,460m] of the mainland) are approved by him much injury will be done to the interests of Portsmouth and vicinity, to the commerce of the Port, particularly in regard to its trade with Southampton, and also that the bye-laws will interfere much with the anchorage and sailing grounds for yachts; and, whether Portsmouth Chamber of Commerce has petitioned against the proposed bye-laws, and other Petitions against them have been sent, he will hold approval of them until he has made a full and careful inquiry as to whether the object to be obtained is of such paramount important to justify him in allowing so serious an interference with the navigation of waters, which from time immemorial have been open to all?*

The President Sir Michael Hicks-Beach *(Bristol West), in reply said he was well aware of the serious objections which had been raised to the bye-laws, and could assure his Hon. Friend that it would not be assented to without full consideration.*

Either the bye-laws were not enacted or they were disregarded, as the following two well-documented and serious incidents illustrate. In September 1890 about 40 or 50 passengers were travelling in a steam launch from Portsmouth to Lee-on-the-Solent and happened to be passing Browndown ranges during a firing session at the butts. A bullet whizzed over the launch, passing between the helmsman and a passenger who were standing about two feet [60cm] apart. Then, in 1925, the steam launch *Culverin* of the Naval Armament Depot at Marchwood, was lying off Browndown when she was struck by bullets from a machine gun which was being fired at the ranges. One bullet penetrated the side of the vessel and struck 17-year-old Sidney White in the neck, necessitating his removal to Haslar hospital for medical attention.

Thirty-five years after the departure of the Anglo-German Legion and without the establishment of a permanent camp, an encampment of huts was built in 1890-1 to the east of the ranges. As well as having huts for both soldiers and officers, a road was also constructed connecting the camp with the Military Road to the Gomer and Elson forts. It is not recorded whether this met with any opposition from the local inhabitants, but it provided a base for the Royal Marines who, in the past, had to march all the way from their barracks at Forton to take part in musketry training.

Between 1893 and 1898, 1,000-yard [915m] ranges and an 800-yard [730m] range were established at Browndown and a 2 ft 6 ins [75cm] gauge railway was laid from a central repairing shop and store, leading to three banks of targets near the shore. The railway trolleys were pushed by hand and the system enabled targets to be moved into position. A further section of railway was added in 1931. After the Second World War, youngsters would often play on any railway trolleys that had been left on this railway line. There were also turntables which diverted the line for each set of target raising areas, and the target raising mechanisms were a source of fun activities for those youngsters.

In 1894, Browndown Halt was built immediately opposite the repairing shop at the rifle ranges on the Fort Brockhurst to Lee-on-the-Solent railway: this provided a most convenient means of moving troops between Fort Gomer to the ranges. The rifle range was a favoured venue for holding service marksmen competitions – in 1899, the Challenge Cup (an inter-services shooting contest) was held at Browndown, and from 1900 onwards the Royal Marines also held their annual shooting cup competition there.

The ranges – and the area to the north of them – were used extensively to train troops in trench warfare during The Great War, and it is still possible to find traces of the trenches that were used. The area to the north was used during the Second World War for live grenade-throwing practice as well as for warfare manoeuvres. Also, during the latter part of, and just after, the Second Word War, the firing range was sometimes used for night-time practice when the target area would be illuminated by parachute flares.

In 1919 there was a proposal to abolish the Royal Marines, but this was rejected by Parliament. Nine years later however, in 1928, the number of Royal Marines was dramatically reduced by over 80 percent: from 55,000 to 9,500. The Royal Marine Artillery and the Royal Marine Light Infantry were amalgamated with the title 'The Royal Marines'. The Light Infantry Barracks at Gosport was closed, and moved to what became the 'Small Arms School' at Browndown, and a permanent building was constructed. The Royal Marines were based and trained at this school during the Second World War, and the area was very much involved in the preparations for D-Day, being designated 'Marshalling Area Camp A19'. The school finally closed in 1957.

Between the Wars, an increasing number of people, including local fishermen, expressed their concerns about the activities on the ranges. In April 1934 they petitioned the Chief Fishery Officer, requesting that action be taken to limit the use of the rifle ranges between the months of November and March, as the ranges covered the area where the fisherman regularly dredged for oysters during those months. The reply, given by Colonel Hatton Budge on behalf of the military, was both robust and exasperated. He pointed out that:
...coast defence Artillery units were being driven from pillar to post, and if every fortification was going to be closed to them, those responsible for the defence of the country would have no means of practice...

A similar response, combined with reminders that the Army was a fundamental arm of the state and, anyway, was at the location first before any of the complainants, was put forward on each occasion that criticism erupted. This rather won the day each time, with the result that there was no particular change in, or curtailment of, the activities on the ranges. With the prevalence of modern health and safety rules and regulations, one suspects that the outcome would be very different were the circumstances to be repeated today.

Another military death was recorded at the camp early in September 1941. A soldier was disembarking from a service lorry with his rifle, on which he had the bayonet fixed. He accidentally knocked the scabbard off and impaled himself on the bayonet, which pierced his left buttock and entered his stomach.

During and after the Second World War, the rifle ranges were an unofficial playground for youngsters when the red flags were not flying. There did not seem to be much of an audit on the ammunition used, because youngsters would go on to the ranges after the soldiers had left and, more often than not, would 'find' rounds of live ammunition. The area was also well-known as a haunt for sailors from Daedalus who would go there when courting their girlfriends, so that youngsters running through the gorse playing 'Cowboys and Indians' would occasionally stumble across the sailors and girlfriends playing 'Doctors and Nurses'.

On the matter of 'finding' live ammunition, some youngsters were a little more proactive in acquiring 'ordnance', as illustrated by the following account. Peter lived with his sister, mother, grandmother and other members of the family in a house in Gosport Road. Before the war, when he was very young, his family had lived at the Number Two Battery at Stokes Bay, and Peter had got to know the layout of the Battery very well but, during the War, that building was used by the army as a munitions store. One day Mr Ross, a special constable, came to the house and asked if Peter lived there. The grandmother, who knew Mr Ross as one of the proprietors of a hardware shop in Lee-on-the-Solent, told him that he did. Mr Ross then said that he believed that Peter, together with others, had 'acquired' some ordnance, to which the grandmother replied "Oh no, that's not the sort of thing Peter would do". The special constable then asked if he might have a look in Peter's room. "Come in," she said, "but you are wasting your time". Under Peter's bed, however, a tin containing hand-grenades was discovered. Peter and his companions had apparently visited the Battery and carried out an acquisition exercise. As a consequence, he and his companions were taken to the police station and were later brought up before the Magistrates who certainly had something to say about it.

Around this time, the Magistrates' Court was quite busy with cases involving youngsters, which is probably why, at a council meeting, a local councillor commented that there were 3,000 children running wild in Gosport. In 1940, a policy of evacuation of school children was introduced locally. Some parents did not agree with this programme and kept their children at home (about half of the 6,000 children in the borough stayed behind), also many of those children who had been evacuated returned home in dribs and drabs by 1942. When the initial evacuation took place some of the vacated schools were taken over and used for different activities such as first aid, rest and training centres and even offices. Consequently education provision became a make-do and often part-time arrangement (older Lee Junior School pupils had lessons in the top floor of the Library and younger ones in a bungalow in Portsmouth Road). Most youngsters were left to their own devices for longer periods of time than had been previously, which inevitably led to an increase in the workload of the Magistrates.

After the Second World War, Browndown reverted to its role as a training area and was used by the 7th Royal Tank Regiment Amphibian Wing, which was based at Fort Gomer. On 7 June 1950, *The Times* reported:

Sir Ouvry Roberts, Commander-in-chief, Southern Command and other British officers observed a demonstration of amphibious warfare given in Stokes Bay. From a D.U.K.W. he saw two un-armoured troop carrying amphibians launched from a landing craft, and two tanks, one a gun tank, made buoyant by canvas structures. As the gun tank reached the beach its guns were brought into action, and a bulldozer from one of the amphibians demonstrated how it could be used in levelling a beach for landing purposes.

These amphibious 'ducks' (DUKWs), which had been used in the Normandy D-day landings six years previously, had proved themselves to be capable of operating in difficult weather conditions. Prior to this, during testing, they had been successfully used in a rescue where there were winds of over 60mph and in rain and heavy surf. The same was not true of the hovercraft that were tested at the Browndown site over a decade later. Although hovercraft can travel over land, sea, mud and ice, they could not match the adverse weather performance of the DUKW. The name of these vehicles is derived from the General Motor Company's model-naming terminology. 'D' shows that it was designed in 1942, 'U' stands for utility, 'K' indicates that it had driven front wheels, and 'W' means that it had two powered rear axles. It is not an acronym for Duplex Universal Karrier Wheeled, as sometimes has been claimed. Although they were designed only to last long enough for combat purposes, and were only built in their original form until 1945, they have proved their worth many times over throughout the world. This was especially true in flood-disaster situations requiring land and water rescues. Even as recently as 2005, they were used in the aftermath of Hurricane Katrina in New Orleans.

Also during the 1950s, Browndown was used by the Royal Marine Forces Volunteer Reserve to train in "station keeping and beaching exercises" – landings which were made from landing craft similar to those observed by Sir Ouvry Roberts.

Although some records state that the 1939 bye-laws for Browndown Ranges allowed the range to be used for anti-tank guns, anti-tank rifles, grenades, machine guns, mortars, revolvers and rifles, no record can be found in *Hansard* regarding such bye-laws. This may have prompted a question in the House of Commons by the local MP in May 1955. It is recorded in *Hansard* as:

5th May 1955

Dr. Bennett *asked the First Lord of the Admiralty if he has ascertained what causes the heavy detonations on the firing range at Browndown that are concussing the local residents and their houses, especially on Friday afternoons, and to whom claims for damage to either should be presented.*

Mr. J.P.L. Thomas: *A record has been kept of all explosions heard on the Range, irrespective of whether or not they originated on it, but it contains no entry in recent months for any heavy explosions. As in the past, the firing of charges during Royal Marine training is only carried out on the part of the range furthest from homes and the maximum weight of these charges is less than 2lbs [1kg]. In the past six months, exercises with explosives have taken place on*

35 days, of which nine have been Fridays. The Major General, Royal Marines, Portsmouth, is always prepared to give close attention to substantiated claims for damage arising from activities in establishments under his command. In the present case, however, it is not considered that any damage could be caused by the relatively small charges fired on the Browndown range.

The problem did not go away, however. As late as 1959, a bungalow in Chester Crescent was hit by an anti-tank rocket thought to have come from the site. The Army was once again fairly robust in its response, stating that there *was no one using that type of missile at Browndown but perhaps it was left behind by a previous unit.* It even went on to suggest that the rocket had been set off by a gardener's bonfire! Although some training continued at Browndown, live firing was suspended for a year between 1977 and 1978 and then resumed.

In 1966 'Hovershow 66' was held at Browndown, at which the new Vickers hovercraft was displayed to the public. In the same year, a Hovercraft Trials Unit, known as the 200 Hovercraft Trials Squadron, was established at Browndown in the area adjacent to the 'Battery'. Two years later, it was renamed 200 Hovercraft Squadron Royal Corp of Transport. A hangar, together with a few other buildings, was built and the top of the Battery was used as an observation post. The trials initially involved the hovercraft SRN6-617; the Saunders Roe's SRN3 was also tested by the British Inter-Service Hovercraft Trials Unit but was never adopted for service. The Trials Unit was disbanded in 1974. Despite their adverse weather unsuitability, hovercraft are still used to great effect throughout the world.

In 1987, the Nature Conservancy Council designated Browndown as a Site of Special Scientific Interest (SSSI) and since then the MoD has held it as a managed conservation area.

In the 1990s, (Special Air Service) Signal Squadron (Reserve), an Army signals unit, was based on part of the site in the vicinity of Browndown Battery. An array of large, high-frequency antennae was erected on the shingle in front of the former Hovercraft hangar. This tall aerial was used for HF communications between the UK and the Balkans during the conflict in that area between 1992 and

1996. There was some local disquiet about the aerial, some believing that it constituted a health hazard, especially after concern had been expressed in the media about perceived dangers of living close to pylons that carried power cables.

By 2009, the camp at Browndown was no longer needed and, in that year, the Ministry of Defence announced its intention to sell it. When bidding closed in December 2010, six offers had been received. The preferred bidder was chosen the following January, but it then took some months of negotiations to bring the sale to a head. In August 2012, it was announced that the campsite had been sold to Jumbuck Ltd for £754.000. The training area at Browndown was not part of the sale but was retained for use by the MoD, with alternative accommodation being arranged for the army cadets using the facility. Gosport Borough Council was quick to point out that it would not countenance the use of the campsite for housing development, as it was part of the strategic gap. With no set plans for redevelopment, Jumbuck Ltd entered into consultations with the planners and there was a suggestion that a leisure operation might be a preferred use.

Nowadays, when the ranges are not in use, the remaining area is open to the public, the Solent Way Coastal Path running through the site alongside the shore.

Browndown made national news once more, on 9 March 2013, when some 200 French soldiers with 43 vehicles, four helicopters, two landing craft and a catamaran, staged a mock invasion of Britain as part of an exercise named 'Mission Jeanne d'Arc'. The 'invasion' exercise took place on the beach and involved a week's training at the site.

On a slightly different aspect it should be noted that the presence of the gorse on Browndown has often led to a number of serious fires, as illustrated by this selection of newspaper reports:

July 1896 − ...*the dry grass along the side of the Lee-on-the-Solent Railway was ignited by sparks from the engine of a passing train. The flames spread rapidly, and soon the furze bushes on the ground behind Browndown huts were blazing. The fire, which raged furiously for hours, devastating a large tract of common land, could be seen from a long distance...About 150 men of the Scottish Rifles and Wiltshire Regiment, stationed at the Ranges for musketry training, were told to extinguish the flames.*

September 1946 – *Exploding ammunition in Gosport gorse blaze. Marines helped by the N.F.S. tackled a large gorse blaze which covered a mock battle area at Browndown ranges. About 10 acres were involved, bullets lost during training operations went off at frequent intervals* [so evidently the scavenging youngsters mentioned above had not found all of the 'misplaced' ammunition]. *No one was injured. Two un-threshed wheat stacks were saved.*

October 1946 – *Browndown gorse fire put out ... after a Verey light used during night operations by the Marines had set fire to an area of gorse. Gosport fire services with the assistance of R.M. firemen successfully fought the fire which threatened a small arms ammunition magazine at Browndown Small Arms depot.*

April 1949 – *Large trees as well as gorse and dense undergrowth roughly three quarters of a square mile were destroyed by a fire at Browndown south-west of an area that is known locally as the "wild grounds"– first concern was to prevent the fire reaching the houses in Portsmouth Road, buildings of the Small Arms School and the hutments at Gomer Camp.*

April 1956 – *Browndown gorse and grass fire threatened the Small Arms School. It raced through 6ft [1.8m] high bamboo grass at the speed of a horse running...over 60 acres extending from the boundary of H.M.S. Siskin airfield to the Small Arms School and Apple Dumpling bridge were burnt out, it also covered part of the Browndown ranges, the old railway track was used as a firebreak. There was a smaller blaze at Portsmouth Road.*

16

THE TRUE STORY OF
DAEDALUS AND ARIEL

The development of early aeroplanes and the formation of the Royal Flying Corps (RFC) in 1912 heralded an entirely new type of warfare. In the run-up to the Great War, the Admiralty was concerned about the measures which should be taken to patrol our coasts, so that an effective system of aerial spotting could be in place. Shore defences could then be provided with advanced warning of any threats of attack or invasion from air or sea.

It was considered that the best means of filling this new reconnaissance role would be the deployment of seaplanes, which were ideal in their ability to be able to land on, and take off from, the waters around the shores rather than being restricted to using airfields. Winston Churchill, as First Lord of the Admiralty, was a particular champion of the use of seaplanes and actively encouraged both the programme generally and the development of the machines.

A naval branch of the RFC existed in the form of The Royal Naval Air Service (RNAS) and later, just before the Great War, this service was separated from the RFC and celebrated its new individual status by flying over the mobilisation fleet in the review at Spithead. The Admiralty, through the RNAS, started creating coastal stations from which the new system of reconnaissance and defence could be operated and co-ordinated. Locally, a seaplane training school was established at Calshot, but it was soon found that this needed to be expanded. Some seaplane trials had already taken place at Lee-on-the-Solent in 1915 and the location was considered to be an ideal site for a new base, as it could provide a quick take-off and return to the beach.

On 30 July 1917, HM Naval Seaplane Training School was opened at Lee-on-the-Solent under the control of the RNAS, on the site of what was later to become HMS Daedalus. This, together with a number of air bases around the south and east coasts, was intended to supplement the coastguard system and provide surveillance to alert our shore defences against sea and air invasion. The base was established as an extension to the seaplane training station at nearby Calshot, at which officers and ratings were trained to fly and maintain seaplanes and flying boats.

The base at Lee-on-the-Solent was initially temporary, comprising Commander D C S Evill, two officers and 30 men, and 30 acres of land which had been requisitioned, along with a number of Victorian houses. Many of the men lived at the base under canvas, while the officers travelled in each day from their billets in Warsash. The first seaplane-training course at Lee commenced on 27 August 1917 with 28 pupils enrolled and the first seaplanes arrived on 22 September of that year.

Among the other aeronautical schools that were established in 1917 was the Special Flying School at Fort Grange, Gosport where, under the command of Major Robert Smith-Barry, the whole character of training for aerial fighting was changed. He had served as CO of No 60 Squadron on the Western Front and his approach to training was based, not on avoiding potentially dangerous manoeuvres (as had been the case up till then), but on exposing trainees to the manoeuvres in a controlled manner so that they could learn to recover from them, gain confidence and become more skilful. This enabled military pilots to fly into action as masters of their aeroplanes.

Smith-Barry's system of training was adopted at Lee-on-the-Solent, with the result that pilots were trained efficiently in a very short period of time. Generally, trainees were allowed to fly solo after just a few hours of dual instruction time. They were then given a second period of dual control, when they were taught aerobatics including loops, spins and rolls. So successful were Smith-Barry's methods that Marshal of the RAF, Lord Trenchard, would later say of him: "The great Smith-Barry! He was the man who taught the air forces of the world to fly."

In 2001, Harlech Television ran a series entitled *Welsh Flying Aces Interviewed* in which Philip Bristow gave his recollections of the RNAS at Lee-on-the-Solent in 1917. He recalled how, at the age of 17, he submitted an application to join the RNAS and was summoned to go before a selection board at its HQ at the Hotel Cecil in The Strand, London. After being selected, he had to buy his own uniform and other items and, a little later, had to make his way to the Royal Naval College in Greenwich. He recalled that, in his intake of recruits, about half were Canadians and half were English.

Although the Royal Navy had a number of flying schools in various parts of the country, he was sent to learn to fly at Vendôme, La Rochelle, France, during the Great War. When he returned to England, he had to report to Lee-on-the-Solent, which he described as a seaplane base on the low cliffs above the Solent, chosen because of its proximity to the larger seaplane base at Calshot where there were float planes and flying boats. The terrain at Lee-on-the-Solent made it possible to make quick take-offs and returns onto the beach. The seaplanes were kept on the cliffs, 20 or 30 feet *[9m]* above the gravel beach onto which they were lowered every morning by a crane and then brought back at night time. During the day, the seaplanes and the small flying boats were kept grounded at the water's edge, floating and tethered to the beach, with a rating taking care of each plane to ensure that it remained secure as the tide changed. When it was time for a plane to fly, the engine would be started and, after the pilot and observer or instructor had got in, it would be pushed off from the shore. The plane would then taxi out some distance and take off into the wind.

Bristow remembered that his time at Lee-on-the-Solent was during late spring and that there was fine weather, giving very good flying conditions with gentle breezes coming from the east. This meant that take-offs were in an easterly direction towards the Pier, upon which a concert party was engaged for that summer season.

Launching in that direction meant that the planes had to taxi out far enough to avoid hitting the pier on take-off.

He also described beginning his training in a dual-control aircraft, with an instructor in front, while he sat in the seat behind. Once the instructor was satisfied with his progress, Bristow was allowed to fly solo, starting with a Short 150 and then moving on to the larger Short 225 which had a large, 12 cylinder Renault Mercedes water cooled engine and a much bigger propeller. Although the controls were similar, the feel was different, and he recalled how there were frequent taking-off and landing practices with different types of aeroplane.

In his description of the aircraft in which he flew, Bristow talked about a small flying boat called an SBA, in which the two occupants sat side by side in the front, with the biplane wings behind and a small rear-facing rotary engine behind the wings. Flying that aircraft was a balancing act, but it was a very pleasant experience when the engine was fully opened up on take-off and the aircraft skimmed along the surface of the water and became airborne. He likened it to being in an open boat with all the world in front of you, as you could not see the wings or the engine, which were behind the pilot.

He recalled with pleasure flying over the Solent and the Isle of Wight, particularly in the early morning, in one of these aircraft, and seeing the sun rise with the beautiful view below. Landing on the water was tricky, as it was necessary to come down in a much steeper approach than was required by other aircraft because, in a front-engined aircraft, the plane was nose heavy and would naturally get into a dive. With the engine and weight behind the cockpit, the SBA had a tendency to lower its tail when power was reduced. When landing, this needed to be counteracted by pushing the controls forward to put the aircraft into a steep glide and then only levelling out when reaching the water. The aircraft would then taxi back to the beach.

When asked how the people of Lee-on-the-Solent felt about being invaded by intrepid young men in flying machines and boats, he replied that they took it in their stride as it was wartime. He added that some of their fine houses on the front had been commandeered, noting that he had a lovely room in a beautiful house on the cliff-top.

After his training was completed at Lee-on-the-Solent and Calshot (which included mock bombings on Fawley Marshes and mock aerial combat with other seaplanes), Bristow was posted to Westgate-on-Sea near Margate.

The temporary base at Lee-on-the-Solent became a permanent station in November 1917 and hangars, workshops, accommodation and a new double slipway were constructed the following September, whereupon the seaplanes were loaded onto trolleys and pushed down the slipway into the water. At sea, the seaplanes would land near the ship and be lifted on board by crane or be lowered to the sea to take-off.

HMS Hermes. This pioneer aircraft carrier took part in King George V's fleet review in the Solent on 26 July 1924. The photograph was taken later that year when she was in Aden. Notice the crane for lifting the aircraft on board and the tarpaulin hangars

On 1 April 1918 the RNAS combined with the RFC to form the RAF and the base became RAF Lee-on-the-Solent. The RNAS Seaplane Training School was transferred to the newly formed RAF on 5 April 1918 and became No 209 Training Station of the RAF. By 1918, the number of personnel at the base had increased to 827 and there were 18 seaplane sheds, eight canvas hangars and 11 slipways.

After the Great War, there was some debate as to whether the base would be retained. It was deliberately run down, as military personnel were demobilised and training ceased completely. Many of the old seaplanes were towed away to Bursledon where they were sold for £5 *[£200]* each. Some of these were converted, with a little ingenuity, into motor-boats. However, the final decision was made in favour of retaining the facility and on 16 June 1919 the RAF & Naval Co-operation School was formed. The name was later simplified to RAF Seaplane School, Lee-on-Solent which, incidentally, represented the first time that the shortened name for the town had been used. By 1920, the base was one of only four naval air stations in the country.

At this time concern was expressed over the RAF's lack of skill in naval spotting and reconnaissance when, during a Fleet Exercise in 1920, RAF observers working with the fleet wrongly reported a group of fishing vessels as a squadron of battleships. Pressure from the Admiralty led to the introduction of trained naval observers within the service, for which special courses were started at Lee on 1 January 1921 and ran until the outbreak of the Second World War. A few years later, on 1 April 1924, the Fleet Air Arm of the RAF was formed. It consisted of those RAF units that were normally deployed on aircraft carriers, fighting ships and shore bases that maintained the aircraft, such as Lee-on-the-Solent.

No 440 Seagull Flight at the Lee Air Base, December 1923

In 1932 the HQ of Coastal Area was moved from central London to Lee-on-the-Solent and this necessitated buying more land behind the seaplane hangars. At the end of September that year the aerodrome was expanded, a grass airstrip was established west of the town and a large building programme was undertaken whereby new residences, a wardroom and hangars were built. The expansion of the airfield did not meet with unqualified approval, as illustrated by an improvised notice displayed in an estate agent's window in the 1930s:

This is Lee on the Solent "Where the rainbow ends"

What to see in our village

Tragic examples of extravagant waste of public money

MAGNIFICENT MANSIONS FOR OFFICERS ONLY known as

Westcliff with fruit & flower gardens Wykeham Hall & grounds

Manor Way Grange with gardeners lodge

18 other Houses NOT for the people

All of these are fitted with Electric light from large private plant

Cinema Playing Fields Tennis Courts Squash Racquet Courts Billiards & Games Room Gymnasium Shoemakers Shop Greenhouses etc etc

The finest Seaside club on the sunny south coast. Entry free with large salaries for Officers only

UPKEEP ENOURMOUS AT TAXPAYERS EXPENSE

Although unsuitable for seaplanes, reconstructed and lengthened slipway is costly and still unsatisfactory

We live here & we know.

Nevertheless, the arrival of aviation was to provide the residents of Lee, and visitors to the resort, with a front-seat view of what was taking place on and above the sea. Not only with regard to the seaplane training but, in 1929 and 1931, Lee-on-the-Solent was the outstanding vantage point from which to observe the internationally acclaimed Schneider Trophy Competition. These events started and finished off

Cowes and there are photographs of the cliff-tops at Lee packed with cars and spectators. In 1935 Sir Alan Cobham's famous 'flying circus' offered members of the public a most rare opportunity to experience a flight over the Solent: one of the highlights of the display was the flight of an 8hp aircraft known as 'The Flying Flea'.

In the mid 1930s, the airfield became linked to a story which was something of a cause célèbre at the time. Dr Herman Görtz entered Britain in August 1935 and quickly teamed up with a 19-year-old German girl called Marianne Emig whom he claimed was his niece. The couple toured around, staying at various locations where airfields were located. At each base, Görtz pretended to paint landscape pictures while taking photographs of the surrounding countryside. Emig, meanwhile, would try to befriend local RAF personnel with a view to extracting what information she could. After the couple had stayed at RAF Mildenhall, they moved on to RAF Manston. While they were staying in Broadstairs, they managed to get acquainted with Kenneth Lewis, a young RAF airman stationed at the Lee-on-the-Solent, who just happened to be on leave and visiting his home in Kent. Emig, playing on the physical attraction which Lewis clearly felt towards her, eventually managed to persuade him to write to her on his return to his base and to send her photographs of RAF aircraft and aerial views of the airfield at Lee-on-the-Solent. Lewis, who was either besotted or naïve, freely complied. After various further escapades in which the activities of the German couple finally came to the attention of the police, Görtz was arrested on his return to England from a trip back to Germany in November 1935 and charged with offences under the Official Secrets Act. His trial at the Central Criminal Court opened on 4 March the following year and was widely reported in the national press. After a strong prosecution case against him, he was found guilty and given a four-year prison term. Emig never returned from Germany and therefore escaped arrest. It is not clear whether Lewis ever faced any charges.

On 14 July 1936, the base at Lee became Coastal Command Headquarters and the nerve-centre of all naval flying, with operational squadrons often using the site. Around this time also, Ross House, a large mansion at the western end of Lee where Marine Parade West turns inland and becomes Stubbington Lane, was incorporated into the base. The property, built in 1898 and known originally as 'Beachcroft', became the official residence of the successive Captains of the base (see also Chapter 26).

The RAF expanded rapidly during the 1930s and in 1938 Parliament decided that the Navy should be granted its own independent air division, the Fleet Air Arm, under the control of the Admiralty. Consequently, on 24 May 1939, the RAF effectively moved out of Lee-on-the-Solent, but many of the personnel remained and were transferred to the Fleet Air Arm, as illustrated by the case of RAF Corporal JW Green (father of one of the authors), who became Petty Officer JW Green based at *HMS Victory* on 20 March 1939 until 23 May 1939, and then on 24 May at HMS Daedalus when the Fleet Air Arm took over.

Corp JW Green in different uniforms following his automatic transfer from RAF to RN

The base was commissioned as the headquarters of Flag Officer Air (Home) under the name HMS Daedalus (after the character who, in Greek mythology, fabricated wings both for himself and his son, Icarus, to enable them to fly). In addition to being the barracks from which Fleet Air Arm personnel were drafted to ships and naval air squadrons, it also became a training centre for telegraphist air gunners (known as 'TAGS'). The site was enlarged to about 500 acres, 400 of which comprised airfield and the remainder used for buildings. This expansion meant that the facility could cater for 100 aircraft.

Shortly after the outbreak of the Second World War, HMS Daedalus became the home of search- and torpedo-attack squadrons and there began a long association with the Fairy Swordfish aeroplanes. These were to prove useful in the strategic attack on the port of Taranto in Italy, as well as on the torpedo strikes against the Bismark. Just along the road from the base, at Hill Head, the Swordfish Hotel took its name from this aircraft. HMS Daedalus became the base of the office of Admiral (Air) and was used extensively during the evacuation of Dunkirk in May/June 1940, with many of the bombing raids on enemy tanks being launched from here following the fall of France. Additionally, its geographical location made it a prime base from which to launch other attacks both in the Channel and on the Continent.

During the Battle of Britain, RN fighters were permanently based at Lee-on-the-Solent and were used to help defend neighbouring towns and cities. Occasionally, visiting RAF units would support them. Of course not all of the action was one way and the base suffered its first air raid on Friday 16 August 1940 when, in the middle of the day, 20 Stuka dive bombers attacked destroying three hangars and 42 aircraft. During this raid, a particular act of heroism emerged. Hurricane fighter pilot Flight Lieutenant James Nicolson of 249 Squadron was engaged in an aerial attack on a Messerschmitt 110 when his plane was hit and caught fire. He remained at the controls and continued attacking before he was finally forced to bale out. He suffered severe wounds and burns to his face and hands and became the only member of Fighter Command to be honoured with the award of a VC.

By June 1942 the limitations of the airfield had become apparent and so a 3,000 ft *[915m]* tarmac runway was laid, backed up by a subsidiary 2,400 ft *[730m]* strip, with blast pens also being built off the perimeter track. At this time the base was very heavily involved with the defence of the Channel, through the deployment of its seaplanes and Swordfish torpedo bombers. In the preparations for D-Day, in addition to the huge accumulation of military hardware and personnel in the town, several Fleet Air Arm Squadrons operated out of HMS Daedalus in support of invasion forces. On 6 June 1944, a record 435 sorties were flown from Lee: no other airfield matched that figure on that day.

Immediately after VE Day, the base took on the role of training in support of the British Pacific Fleet in the war in the Far East, although this conflict was, of course, foreshortened by the surrender of Japan after the dropping of the atomic bombs.

Following the end of all hostilities, HMS Daedalus continued as an air station and still had an important role to play supporting operations in the Korean War, the Suez Crisis, Aden and the Indonesian conflicts. The seaplane facilities closed and the slipway was abandoned in 1946, but the base became the home of the 1st Fleet Air Arm Field Gun Crew in 1947. This crew became famous, among other things, for their appearances at Royal Tournaments. At about the same time, the base became one of the first naval establishments to operate helicopters.

During the 1953 Coronation fleet review, HMS Daedalus was used as a temporary base for many of the 327 naval aircraft which took part and was responsible for overall control of the whole formation flypast.

In July 1954 a very unusual and most unfortunate accident happened at the base. Enda Andrew Michael Fitzpatrick (18), a naval airman based at Lee, was limbering up by running on foot around the perimeter track at the airfield, when he accidentally strayed into the path of some naval pedal-cyclists who were racing in the area. He collided with one of the cyclists and, tragically, he died later at Haslar Hospital from the injuries he sustained.

On 31 October 1959, the base was renamed HMS Ariel when it became a ground training establishment and the Royal Naval Air Engineering School moved here from Worthy Down (before moving on again to HMS Sultan in 1995). The name reverted to HMS Daedalus in 1965 and the base became the home of 781 Squadron, the Search and Rescue Flight. Around this time, and up to and including the 1970s, the Naval Hovercraft Trials unit was based here. It was an ideal site, especially after works were carried out to widen and improve the old seaplane slipway, although this was not the first association between Lee and the invention of the hovercraft. In 1962, the Inter Service Hovercraft Trials Unit was formed at Lee and was undertaking hovercraft tests the following year. To this day the base remains the home of the Hovercraft Museum (see Chapter 25).

Aircraft old and new at HMS Daedalus base, 1960s

A memorable day in the history of the base was 20 May 1966, when the Fleet Air Arm was presented with the freedom of the Borough of Gosport. About 800 officers, ratings and WRNS proudly paraded through Gosport to receive the award. Later, in 1970, the Air Mechanical Engineering School was transferred to HMS Daedalus from Arbroath and, by this time, the base was losing its former importance and status and many of its operations were transferred to RNAS Yeovilton.

In the early 1980s, operational use was being run down quite rapidly, although there was one swansong in April 1982 when a huge number of helicopters, Harriers and various other RN aircraft used HMS Daedalus while joining ships or supplying the Task Force during the Falklands Crisis.

Notwithstanding such decline, the base was still the focus of much local and national attention especially when, in quick succession in the early 1980s, it hosted visits by three very different and intriguing celebrities – although none of them in human form. On 16 April 1980, Richard Noble's *Thrust 2* jet-powered car was unveiled and completed a test run at the airfield and, three days later, made its first high-speed run at the Daedalus Air Day. Powered by a Rolls-Royce Avon engine taken from a Lightning Fighter, the car went on to take the world land-speed record on 4 October 1983 at a speed of 633.468mph (although, needless to say, not at Lee-on-the-Solent!)

Another celebrated machine to come to the base around this time was the ex-Antillies Air Boat, Short Sandringham, Southern Cross. Weighing 19 tons and having a wingspan of 113ft *[34m]*, it was the largest aircraft to use the slipway when it was taxied across the Solent and brought ashore at Lee on 9 July 1981. Plans to return it to use for commercial pleasure-trips were dashed when funds could not be raised to restore it to flying condition. It left Lee on 1 March 1983 to become the centrepiece of the display at the Southampton Hall of Aviation.

In the skies above Lee in 1983, the local population was able to witness a spectacle which was truly a case of history repeating itself. During the Arms Exhibition at Whale Island that summer, an airship owned by Airship Industries was based at HMS Daedalus and made a number of flights from the airfield. At 150 ft *[45m]* long and carrying 12 passengers and two crew, it provided a fascinating reminder of the times many years before when a Zeppelin, and later the R100, travelled through the same airspace.

In February 1983, the role of the Fleet Air Arm Search and Rescue was assumed by Wessex 772 Squadron, before coming under civilian control in March 1988. The base was by now considerably depleted and a shadow of its former self, apart from when it hosted the popular HMS Daedalus public open days (the last of which was held in 1995) and performed a major part in the D-Day commemorative celebrations in 1984 and 1994. It finally closed in 1996.

The Hampshire Police Air Support Unit then took over the daily management of the site, which continued to be used by various parties who had been present before closure. These included two flying schools, some private aircraft, the Portsmouth Naval Gliding Club, The Lee Bees Model Flying Club, The Tigers Children's Motorcycle Display Team and the Hovercraft Museum.

When, in 2003, the government announced proposals to use some of the buildings within the former base to house asylum seekers, local residents immediately formed the Daedalus Action Group to oppose the scheme. The Group rapidly acquired a large and active membership which organised protest rallies and marches around the town, lobbied the local MP, voiced its concerns direct to government officials and delivered a large petition to Downing Street. On 3 February 2004, the government announced its decision to abandon the proposal and the Group held a large celebration rally on the seafront. Shortly afterwards Channel 4 broadcast a *Dispatches* television documentary entitled *Keep Them Out* which had been filmed in the town and showed the issues arising over the previous few months. Daedalus Action Group continued to monitor the site for a further four years before disbanding in September 2008.

Ownership of the site was divided in March 2006. The Maritime and Coastguard Agency held the runways and surrounding areas for continued use by its own rescue helicopters and for the local police aircraft to operate (the Hampshire Police Air Support Unit being one of the tenants of the Agency). Private groups also used the runways. The remaining areas, including many of the buildings and hangars, came under the control of the South East England Development Agency (SEEDA) which soon issued a statement saying: *The lack of availability of serviced employment land and new business space has been identified as an important requirement in South Hampshire. Our intention is that development of the site will focus on new aviation and marine related businesses, exploiting access to existing runways and the Solent. Plans are to create a quality business location that will attract inward investment and provide accommodation for start-up, growing and established businesses.* In line with this policy, various aviation-related businesses, a flying school and a number of private aircraft owners became tenants on the site.

The 400 acres covered by the whole site straddles the Gosport and Fareham Boroughs, and the two local authorities issued a Joint Planning Statement for Daedalus in April 2006. In it they stated that there should be leisure and community elements developed on the land to complement existing facilities and benefit local residents. The statement also emphasised that any future development undertaken should maximise the use of the runways for general and private aviation purposes.

The following month, general repairs were being carried out to the runways when 20 unexploded Canadian pipe mines were discovered. The mines were up to 65 ft *[20m]* long and had been buried under the airfield during the Second World War to be detonated in the event of a German invasion, thereby rendering the airfield unusable. The mines discovered represented the last of the original 265 originally planted and each contained up to 2,400 lbs *[1,080kg]* of explosives. They were removed over five weeks in September and October 2006 and this involved the systematic and periodic evacuation of up to 900 homes near the area, making it the largest ever peacetime evacuation in Britain. Once retrieved, the mines were destroyed by controlled explosion. This was not the first time that such an event had occurred. Between 16 and 27 October 1989, a smaller evacuation was carried out to allow the retrieval of 13 buried pipe mines under a programme named 'Operation Minotaur'. All were successfully removed and only one was found to be live on that occasion.

On 18 October 2007, notice was given to all users of the airfield that the site would close and only be available for use by the Maritime and Coastguard Agency, the Hampshire Police Air Support Unit and the Portsmouth Naval Gliding Club. The closure was due to take place on 16 November 2007, but the Lee Flying Association and a group of other parties managed to make a successful challenge to the proposal by developing new operating procedures. The airfield therefore continued in use for general aviation, with various aviation-related businesses being based there.

In August 2011, the government designated the site as one of 11 enterprise zones around the country, and businesses that decided to invest there could benefit from discounted rates and guaranteed superfast broadband. The vision was to transform the area into *a thriving location for the benefit of existing residents, businesses and the local economy bringing the whole site into productive use whilst being sensitive to its historic land use, the listed buildings and the designated conservation area.* The following year, ownership of much of the site passed to the Homes and Community Agency, which ran the development programme with the Solent Local Enterprise Partnership and the Partnership for Urban South Hampshire. Britten Norman took over the management of the site. It was envisaged that development would be carried out in phases and that between 38 and 45 businesses would be set up on the site.

The Fareham and Gosport Borough Councils unanimously approved an outline planning application in March 2012 to enable the development proposals to proceed. It was estimated that this would bring about 4,000 jobs to the area, mostly in the marine and aerospace fields. The outline planning permission also paved the way for 164 new homes (the MOD had in fact built 148 married quarters on the site some years before), a sheltered housing development, some shops, allotments and a 34-acre public open space.

In 2013, Fareham College published its plans for the development of a new Centre of Excellence for Engineering, Manufacturing and Advanced Skills Training aimed at helping students gain skills to enable them to get employment. It was envisaged that the facility would cater for 600 students in classrooms and workshops with a café and two playing pitches. Work also started to improve the access roads onto the site. The route of one of these runs south directly opposite Marks Road in Stubbington and therefore follows part of the route of the old original road into Lee which existed for a very long time before the airfield development swept it away. It is, as the French might say, a case of 'plus ça change, plus c'est la même chose.'

Of course, with the arrival of flying in the area, incidents and accidents were almost inevitable, as these reports through the years show:

September 1921 – *A seaplane when about to land a mile from the shore at Lee-on-the-Solent suddenly nose-dived and was wrecked. The two occupants were rescued by a motor launch.*

July 1923 – *A new type of aeroplane came to grief in a field at Lee on-the-Solent yesterday and Pilot Officer Wake was killed. The machine was completely smashed.*

January 1925 – *An aeroplane stationed at Fort Grange, Gosport, crashed on the Lee-on-Solent golf links this morning and turned over on its back. The nose of the machine was damaged and the propeller blade broken off, but the pilot escaped injury.*

September 1925 – *During flying exercise over Lee-on-Solent an aeroplane, piloted by Flight-Lieut. G.A. Cavis-Brown, suddenly spun around and then nose-dived, crashing to earth from 500ft [150m]. The machine was totally wrecked and the pilot terribly injured, death occurring before his admission to hospital. The Air Ministry announces that the aeroplane was a Blackburn-Blackburn machine, of R.A.F. Base Gosport. The pilot who lost his life was the sole occupant of the aircraft.*

October 1945 – *A corporal in the R.A.F. stationed in Gosport was killed in a Swordfish practising torpedo launching in collision with a Beaufighter. This was believed to be off Stokes Bay.*

February 1946 – *Two pilots were killed when two naval aircraft collided in mid air – locked together and crashed into a field of Common Barn owned by Mr. C. House near to the R.N.A.S. The planes were an Avro Anson and a De Haviland Domine, and the accident occurred at 11.15 in the morning.*

The worst local air crash in terms of loss of life did not involve an airplane from Daedalus, but happened a few hundred yards offshore in the Solent, near where the Belle Vue Hotel was then situated. In February 1946, a Sunderland flying boat belonging to Coastal Command came down a little to the east of Lee-on-the-Solent pier at 4.30am. It had taken off from Calshot at 4.26am en route for Augusta in Sicily and Karachi, and, shortly after take off, had reported by radio that one of its engines had broken down and that there had been an explosion. Residents in a top-floor flat in Marine Parade said the heavy explosion awakened them. One witness recounted that she and her husband could see the flying-boat in flames from their window. Water was poured on to the blazing aircraft for almost four hours but it sank just after 8am. Ten airmen lost their lives in the crash and the shoreline was littered with wreckage.

The following year, a crash at the Air Display cast a shadow over the complete show:

July 1947 – *Inquest on the air show crash. The Pilot was warned not to do any aerobatics, but in spite of that, he attempted to do a roll and crashed. He was told to carryout a fly past to demonstrate a Blackburn Firebrand carrying a torpedo. After taking off he came over the aerodrome at about 50ft [15m] and when at the eastern end pulled up to about 200ft [60m] and started to execute a roll. While in the inverted position he started to lose height. There appeared to be an attempt to right the aircraft and it disappeared from view. He was single and 22 years old.*

Other tragedies were reported locally:

November 1949 – *Air crash at Lee. A road worker who was working in a manhole in Stubbington Lane was crushed when a plane overran the runway and appeared to turn a complete somersault. The pilot was also killed.*

April 1950 – *Civilian Auster aircraft crashed at the western end of Stokes Bay.*

Also in April 1950 – *A pilot (with D.F.C.) was killed in a Sea Hornet when it crashed on the north side of the station's perimeter behind two cottages in Gosport Road, Stubbington. He was demonstrating an air loop to cadets.*

August 1955 – *At 10.45pm an Avenger aircraft crashed on the sea during a landing exercise after its engine had cut out, the three members of the crew were OK, one was taken to Haslar Hospital for observation. Mrs. Joan Titheridge, in her night-dress, helped her husband with their dingy he, Peter Titheridge of 41 Marine Parade West, rowed out to the aircraft.*

August 1955 – *A Miles Magister crashed at a field near Court Barn Farm.*

October 1955 – *Vampire jet overshot the runway and crossed Stubbington Lane and ended up in rough ground. Motorist Mr. T. Seden of 2 Maple Close and another motorist released the occupants who were unhurt.*

17

SEAGULLS OVER
THE SOLENT

We have seen how, during the Great War, Lee-on-the-Solent was very important in providing both training and a base in the use of early seaplanes. After the Armistice, Supermarine continued designing and building seaplanes with great success, with R J Mitchell becoming its chief designer in 1920.

The SBA seaplane, which Philip Bristow described in the previous Chapter, was a forerunner of the Supermarine Walrus, a single-engine amphibious biplane designed by R J Mitchell and first flown in 1933. Developed initially for use as a fleet spotter plane to be catapult-launched from cruisers or battleships, the Walrus was later employed in a variety of other roles, which included use as a rescue aircraft for aircrews that had 'ditched' and was used throughout the Second World War.

With the engine facing the rear (that is, pusher configuration) the Walrus had the advantage of keeping the engine and propeller out of the way of spray when operating on water, as well as reducing noise level within the aircraft. It was also safer for any member of the crew who had to stand on the front deck, for example when picking up a mooring line, as they would not be near the rotating propeller. When on operations from a warship, the Walrus would be catapulted from the ship and, on returning from a flying mission, it would be recovered by touching-down alongside the ship, to be lifted from the sea by a ship's crane. A member of the Walrus crew would climb onto the top wing and attach the crane hook, a procedure hardly more hazardous than picking up a mooring line.

It was discovered early on, however, that the Walrus had a tendency to yaw. This was caused by unequal forces on the rudder resulting from the vortex produced by the propeller. To correct this, the engine was offset by three degrees to starboard. The first prototype Walrus was flown by 'Mutt' Summers on 21 June 1933 and, just five days later, made an appearance at an air show at Hendon where pilot Summers startled the spectators, including R J Mitchell, when he looped the loop. This was only possible because the aircraft had been strengthened to enable it to be launched by catapult. The robustness of the Walrus was illustrated in 1935 when the pilot, landing on water, forgot that the undercarriage was down and the Walrus flipped over completely. All of those on board, including the commander-in-chief of the Home Fleet, Admiral Roger Backhouse, escaped with only minor injuries. The aircraft was later repaired and returned to service but it is not known what the Admiral said to the pilot!

The Walrus was affectionately known as the 'Shagbat' or sometimes 'Steam-pigeon', the latter name coming from the steam produced by water striking the hot Pegasus engine. Perhaps the nickname 'Shagbat' comes from the way the seaplane breasted the waves when on the water, in the majestic manner of a cormorant or shag immortalised in the nonsense rhyme, by Christopher Isherwood:

The common cormorant or shag

Lays eggs inside a paper bag.

The reason you will see, no doubt,

It is to keep the lightning out.

But what these unobservant birds

Have never noticed is that herds

Of wandering bears may come with buns

And steal the bags to hold the crumbs.

Possibly, when the aircraft was in the air, it tended to adopt the more erratic flight patterns of a bat. Whether or not this is how the

Walrus got its nickname can only be speculated, but it certainly would not be any modern connotation and there is usually there is some reason behind a nickname.

Just after the beginning of the Second World War, two Walruses were used at Lee-on-the-Solent for trials of ASV (Air to Surface Vessel) radar. This technology was in its infancy and the system that was tested used a pair of dipole aerials mounted on the struts between the aircraft's wings. In 1940, an experiment was carried out which involved the mounting of a forward-firing Oerlikon 20mm cannon, for use against German E-boats. Unfortunately the muzzle flash was so bright that the pilot soon became blinded and the idea was abandoned.

The successor to the Walrus, and of similar but more powerful design, was the Supermarine Sea Otter. This never completely replaced the Walrus but served alongside it in the air-sea rescue role during the latter part of the War. A post-war replacement for both aircraft, the Supermarine Seagull, was cancelled in 1952, with only prototypes being constructed and therefore, unlike Sorrento, the Solent was not to keep Seagulls. By that time, helicopters were taking over from small flying-boats in the air-sea rescue role.

A discussion of seaplanes and Lee-on-the-Solent would not be complete without reference to the Schneider Trophy competitions, which will be examined in the next Chapter. Between 1926 and 1931 R J Mitchell's interest in the Schneider Trophy can be seen in the seaplanes that he designed. When one compares pictures of the Sealion II (1920) and the Seagull II (1924) with the S5 and S6/S6B (1926-1931) it really is a case of the ugly duckling becoming a beautiful swan. Within a few years this graceful design went on to become embodied in the most graceful fighter plane – the Spitfire.

18

ON CLOUD NINE

It is difficult to overstate the extent to which the Schneider Trophy competitions of the inter-war years captured the nation's interest and excitement. National pride and fervour reached particularly high levels in 1929 and 1931 when the competition was held over the Solent – and Lee-on-the-Solent was at the centre of the excitement. Before examining how our area became the focus of the nation at those times, it may be useful to set the matter in context by taking an overall look at the background and history of the competition.

On 5 December 1912, Jacques Schneider (1879-1928), a French aviation enthusiast, announced that he was instigating a new competition aimed at encouraging manufacturers to achieve advances in aircraft technology. From his own funds he financed the production of a beautiful silver trophy which was to be presented to the winning nation. The competition (officially named 'Coupe d'Aviation Maritime Jacques Schneider') was open to any nation which wished to compete and each nation (club) could enter up to three aeroplanes. Each aircraft had to fly a basically triangular course of 150 miles, but also be in contact with the sea for a minimum of 547 yards [500m]. The aeroplane completing the course in the fastest time would be the winner and the winning nation, in addition to holding the Trophy until the next competition, would have the honour of hosting the following year's event. The competition would end when any of the competing nations won the Trophy on three occasions within a five-year period and the winner would then get to keep the Trophy permanently. The winning pilot on that occasion would also receive a substantial cash prize.

The first competition was on 16 April 1913 at Monaco and was won by the French.

In 1914 it was held at Monaco once again when victory went to Britain.

After a break for the duration of the Great War, the competition resumed and was held in 1919 at Bournemouth where, unfortunately, weather conditions were particularly poor. Dense fog hampered speed measurement and it was very difficult for both the public and the pilots to see. Probably as a result of this, only one aeroplane – an Italian entrant – completed the course, but was later disqualified due to the pilot making an error in turning at the wrong point. In the end, the whole competition that year was declared void and the Italians were placated in part by being allowed to host the event next time around.

At Venice in 1920 the Italians were unopposed and so won the competition.

In 1921 the event was held at Venice once again. The course distance was increased to 212 miles and the Italians achieved a second successive victory, putting them one win away from claiming the Trophy for all time.

Naples was the host for the 1922 competition, at which Italian hopes were high and a crowd of about 25,000 gathered to watch. The British only entered one aeroplane, a Supermarine Sea Lion II designed by R J Mitchell. With this, they narrowly won, thus ensuring the continuance of the competition for at least another year. Tragically, an Italian pilot crashed and was killed. After that year's competition, the rules were changed slightly so that, immediately before competing, each aircraft had to sit in the water moored to a buoy for six hours without any human intervention. The aircraft was then required to be flown subject to any problems arising as a result of this new rule, such as any water taken in through leaks.

Following victory at Naples, Britain hosted the next year's competition in 1923 when it was held over the Solent just off Cowes. The USA, however, denied the host nation any glory.

In 1924 the event was due to be held in the USA, but none of the other nations was ready to field any aeroplanes. In view of this, the Americans rather sportingly agreed that the competition should be held over from that year to the next.

Baltimore was the setting for the 1925 competition, at which the Americans had a home win. Around this time, the event was beginning to acquire nationalist political undercurrents, especially when the government of Fascist Italy began to take a direct involvement in the proceedings. In both Britain and the USA austerity meant that military funding was being reduced and the British were dependent on a combination of aircraft manufacturers and commercial and private sponsors for the financial support necessary both to develop ever more technologically advanced aircraft and to enter the competition generally. However, Benito Mussolini's government was enthusiastic in its financial support of its manufacturers and developers and Il Duce himself had announced that the Trophy would be claimed by Italy in 1926 come what may.

Supermarine's chief engineer, R J Mitchell, had not been able to get Britain's entry ready for the 1926 competition, which was held at Hampton Roads, USA. The Italians were indeed victorious once more and again stood to retain the Trophy if they could secure another victory in the next three years. British resolve to stop this happening hardened considerably – it became a matter of politics, pride and 'bulldog- determination to kill Mussolini's dream.

By 1927, the event had become one of the most celebrated and prestigious air competitions in the world. Schneider's original vision had been to encourage advancements in aero-engineering, and there was no doubt that this was certainly being achieved, but most of the public viewed the competition as a test of pure speed as well as national pride. The average winning speed had risen from a mere 45.71 mph in 1913 to 246.49 mph in 1926. The event was now attracting huge crowds (in 1926 there were 200,000 spectators) and creating a holiday atmosphere. Back in Venice once again in 1927, the British – who were ready this time round – were victorious with a Supermarine S6B and an average winning speed of 281.66 mph.

Jacques Schneider died in 1928 and it was decided that the competition would henceforth be held every other year, in order to allow each competing club more time to develop new technical advances.

So now we come to 1929 when, once again, Britain would host the competition and this time it was to be held in the Solent, with Lee providing a ringside seat.

The course for the 1929 competition started off West Cowes and ran down to a turn off Nettlestone Point on the Isle of Wight. It then followed a line to a mark buoy due south of Hayling Island before turning again to a point just off Southsea. From there it ran due west right over Gilkicker point (the only area of land over which the aircraft flew) to complete the circuit back at a mark buoy north of West Cowes. Only Great Britain and Italy entered teams (of three aircraft each). France was unable to enter a team and the United States proposed entrant failed to participate. It was widely anticipated that one of the British machines would set a new world speed record.

Such was the interest in the event that special coaches and trains were laid on to bring spectators in. The Prince of Wales flew from London to Calshot and the Prime Minister left for Cowes by road. In the national press, the RAC issued notices announcing that it had made car parks available at Portsmouth, Gosport, Lee-on-the-Solent and Hayling Island which could collectively accommodate 10,000 cars. The prices in these car parks varied from 2s 6d *[£6]* to £1 *[£48]* according to their position. At Lee, spaces in the more highly priced enclosures could be booked in advance. Additionally, the RAC announced that it had been able to reserve for its members and associate members the use of the pier at Lee, admission to which cost £1 *[£48]*, although *special reductions in the prices for parking cars will be made to holders of tickets to the pier balcony*. One press correspondent wrote: *I should fancy it will only be those motorists who are early on the scene…who will find any place to spare within these reservations. Spectators who were able to install themselves some days ago on the Isle of Wight tell me that delightful resort can now best be described by the phrase "Tight little island".*

One can get a sense of the atmosphere around our area from newspaper reports of the time. A good summary was provided from as far afield as *The Dundee Courier* in its edition of 9 September 1929:

Never has this country seen such an amazing crowd as gathered on the shores of the Solent to witness the great race.

Noon saw a huge concourse of people taking all roads that led to the seashore. Stands were filled with men in cool flannel suits and women dressed in brilliantly coloured frocks and carrying parasols as some protection against the almost tropical heat and brilliant sun glare.

Thousands of picnic parties were to be seen along the miles of front.

Large crowds lined the fringes of Stokes Bay and another dense throng gathered on the beach at Lee-on-Solent.

Southsea woke in the morning to find that its population had doubled during the night, and that tens of thousands of people were still pouring into the town.

Mothers with young children had been found shelter in corporation buildings, schools, and drill halls, and officials had provided sacking in lieu of blankets for those who needed them.

Certain roads had to be closed to all but food lorries and official cars. But for this the vast multitude could never have been fed.

Even the most expert observers gazed at the passing road traffic in amazement. For mile after mile bicycles, tiny cars, great saloons and mammoth motor coaches ran end to end.

It was estimated that a hold-up of 30 seconds at any point on a main road near Portsmouth meant the stopping of vehicles for a mile back. It was like Derby Day and the cup final in one as far as the traffic was concerned.

Up in the air, both of the Italian aeroplanes developed problems while in flight but managed to land safely. The British machines took first and second places, although the latter was subsequently disqualified as the pilot had flown inside part of the course. Thus the Italians took second place, but with a speed over 44 mph slower than the winner. The winning entry was a Supermarine S6, which reached an average speed of 328.64 mph.

By 1931, the British government had withdrawn all funding for the Supermarine entries, but Lady Lucy Houston came to the rescue by putting up £100,000 *[£5,450,000]* to save the day and the competition returned to the Solent in 1931. Once again it was a straight contest between the British and the Italians, the French entry not being ready in time. One Italian pilot crashed in trials and was killed, prompting the Italians to lodge a request to Britain to postpone the event. This was refused. With the Italians having withdrawn from the competition, a third and final British win was inevitable. Although the lack of competition meant that some of the enthusiasm seen in 1929 had evaporated, there was still much interest in the event, especially in seeing if a new world record could be set.

Once again the RAC was busy. It produced a special map showing recommended routes to the principal destination points adjacent to the course, with each point being given a distinctive colour. Destination badges matching the colours were given to motorists, so that each car could be directed without delay to the appropriate point. The colours for Lee-on-the-Solent were white on green. Additionally, the RAC erected hundreds of special signposts on all main roads leading to the destination points and had a large number of guides and patrols available throughout the day to direct and control traffic and to render assistance in cases of breakdown. Many coach excursions were laid on to the chief vantage points of Southsea, Portsmouth, Gosport, Hayling Island, Lee-on-the-Solent, Stokes Bay, Alverstoke and the Isle of Wight. Special trains ran from London to Portsmouth and huge car parks were once again organised. The flying area was closed to all shipping from 11am.

Although originally scheduled for 12 September, the event had to be postponed to the following day due to bad weather. On 13 September, the only two machines, both Supermarine S6Bs, took off from Lee-on-the-Solent for the 217½ mile course. It was estimated that the number of spectators approached one million. Flight Lieutenant John Boothman did not disappoint them and completed the course with a winning average speed of 340.08 mph, setting a new world record and making the Supermarine the fastest aeroplane in the world.

Lee had seen days of glory, the competition came to an end, the Schneider Trophy was retained permanently in Britain and is now in the Science Museum in London.

There was one more occasion, just 17 days later, when Lee-on-the-Solent was in the national news again. On 29 September 1931, Flight Lieutenant C H Stainforth broke the air-speed world record in six runs over a course from Lee-on-the-Solent to Hill Head. He was flying the same Vickers Supermarine seaplane which had claimed the Schneider Trophy earlier that month, but which had since been refitted with a new Rolls Royce 'Sprint' engine. The flight was timed by electrical camera apparatus at each end of the course, accurate to one millionth part of a second, and the film was developed by officials at Lee-on-the-Solent, who were able to issue confirmation to the nation early the following morning that an average speed of 408.8 mph had been achieved. The log showed that visibility was so poor that Stainforth could only steer by the formation of the clouds and when news of the new world record reached him he was playing shove-halfpenny in the officers' mess at Calshot. "I thought I had done it," he calmly observed … and then went on playing his game.

19

BLOOD, TOIL, TEARS AND SWEAT

As mentioned in Chapter 16, the first air raid at Lee-on-the-Solent took place on Friday 16 August 1940. Five of the people killed were civilians, two of whom were in a bakery van which was being driven along Marine Parade West on its delivery round when it became the target of machine-gun fire. Records show that Cecil Grout (15) of 32 Elmore Avenue was one of those killed. He was working for the Browning Bakery in Lee-on-the-Solent and the van was being driven by Geoffrey Browning, son of Beatrice Browning, the owner of the bakery. Geoffrey was badly injured and was taken to Gosport War Memorial Hospital, where he died that same day.

After that time, air raids generally took place at night. People would huddle in the dark, mostly in silence, listening to the drone of German bomber squadrons flying high above on their way to targets elsewhere in the country. All those sheltering from the raids would be hoping that it was not going to be their turn that night, but of course there were the times when it was their turn.

In a night raid on HMS Daedalus on 23 November 1940, ten WRNS were killed when a stray anti-aircraft shell penetrated the roof and exploded in the dining room of their billet just outside the base at Mansfield House in Newton Place (see Appendix 4). Eight of them were buried in Haslar Cemetery. At the site where they perished, there is a plaque near the front door commemorating this tragic event.

On January 10 1941, there was a fire blitz in the Portsmouth area. Some 3,000 people were made homeless and 170 were killed. There was also a concentrated air attack on Gosport that night.

In one of the last air raid alerts of the War, on 16 May 1944, an anti-aircraft shell fell on the vicarage of St Faith's Church. The shell hit the corner of the bedroom in which the vicar, Rev Douglas Egbert Hunter, was sleeping. He was thrown across the room and later died on his way to Haslar Hospital. His wife, who was in another part of the property at the time, was only slightly injured. Aged 60, Rev Hunter had been shortly due to retire and was a much respected and well-liked member of the community who had worked tirelessly within the parish. His ashes were interred close to the south porch of the church.

During the raids, a large anti-aircraft gun, which became known locally as 'Big Tom', could be heard. It was situated at the edge of the Warren and the site of it can still be found. Take the track across the Warren near the traffic lights at the eastern end of Lee and follow it down the dip and up the slope on the far side, then walk about a hundred yards [90m], keeping to the left near the boundary of the Warren. Up to a few years ago it was still possible to find remnants of the gun emplacement.

Between 1940 and 1944, there were 61 air raids on the Gosport peninsula in which 111 people were killed, 289 were wounded and many properties were badly damaged. Among all the dreadful happenings there were occasional lighter moments, as the following episode illustrates. In Brickland Terrace lived a Mrs P, who had several small children and was either a widow or had a husband serving somewhere in the War. She was one of the few people in the area at the very beginning of the War who had an Anderson shelter and she allowed other families to share it. On the fateful day of Friday 16 August 1940, the air-raid siren had sounded and several neighbouring families were crammed in the shelter with her and her family. An aerial dogfight started and was taking place more or less immediately above that part of Lee-on-the-Solent. In the house, it turned out that there was a sailor 'friend' who had, as we say nowadays, 'slept over' at Mrs P's. Perhaps because he wanted to show how 'macho' he was, he had not gone down to the air-raid shelter when the siren had sounded and had decided to stay in the house but, more likely, he had preferred not to show his face to the inquisitive ladies of the neighbourhood. However, the dogfight became rather noisy and intense and, at the last minute, 'Jolly Jack' decided to make a dash for the shelter and literally dived in. Unfortunately, in doing so, he caught his back on the corrugated iron on the top of the doorway, cried out and fell on to the concrete floor. Although not seriously injured, he was in some pain and thought that he had been hit by the gunfire. Believing he was dying, he made what he thought was his final confession concerning his wife in Plymouth and the extramarital activities in which he and Mrs P had indulged … it was not long after this that Mrs P moved away from the area, never to be heard of again. One of the authors was in fact in the shelter at that time.

To boost morale and aid the War effort, youngsters were encouraged to collect waste paper and, when they had collected a certain amount, they were rewarded with free entry tickets to the cinema. Another morale booster in February 1942 was a visit by Lt Cdr Ralph Richardson, during which he toured Lee-on-the-Solent with a mobile cinema van, towing large-scale models of a torpedo boat and submarine. A concert and film show at Lee Tower Cinema and a dance at Lee Tower Ballroom followed – the stated aim being the raising of money for the War effort. The Tower ballroom was often the location of morale-boosting events around this time. In 1942, balls and dances were held there on behalf of the Red Cross and organised by Mr Ralph West, a local builder who lived in Portsmouth Road. Sadly just three years later, in July 1946, a boat in which he was sailing off Browndown capsized due to strong winds and tides and he died of the effects of shock and exposure, aged 53.

When not scavenging for 'misplaced' ammunition, youngsters – if they were able to get onto the beach – would go beachcombing. The coveted finds were K rations, which were a day's pre-packed food issued to soldiers fighting at the Front. After D-Day, they could be found on the foreshore when ships had been sunk, and because of the rationing and general shortage of food, these finds were particularly prized. The K rations consisted of packets measuring about 4 ins by

8 ins by 1½ ins *[10cm by 20cm by 3cm]* in waterproof packaging. The outsides were often coated with tar, but the contents would still be still intact. Although there was more than one type, in general they contained a small can of meat, biscuits, sweets (glucose tablets), a dried fruit bar, a pack of four cigarettes, a strip of matches, chewing gum, a packet of instant coffee, a packet of sugar, and a sachet of powdered lemon drink.

One popular feature during the War was the voluntary canteen set up by Mrs Lloyd-Jones for the servicemen. She was ably assisted by a number of young girls who gave up their time for no reward, in order to help as waitresses or do the washing up.

By the time D-Day came, the beach was cordoned off with barbed wire. At the time of the 1944 fleet review (see Chapter 23) some of the servicemen who embarked on the ships taking part in the review were encamped on the cliffs at Lee-on-the-Solent. The Canadians were situated between the sailing club and the Old Ship public house, the British were located between the Belle Vue Hotel and Lee Tower, and the Americans were based on the other side of the Tower.

The Canadians had an improvised notice facing the road at the junction of Portsmouth Road and Marine Parade East which read:

BABY SITTING FOR FEMALES
AGED 8 TO 80

While this caused some amusement and outrage in equal measure, it is not known if there were any takers!

Shortly after D-Day, there were still military personnel in the area and, on the cliffs opposite what was then the Belle Vue Hotel, the army had a large marquee in which troops were served their meals. Here, occasionally, local youngsters were also given buns and mugs of tea sweetened with condensed milk.

20
WHEN THE LIGHTS CAME ON AGAIN

At the end of the War in Europe there was great rejoicing: anyone who was around at that time will remember the VE Day celebrations, especially as nearly every road held a street party. Although there had been no air raids for a long time, it was not until after VE Day that people no longer had to bother about the blackout. Lights were switched on, curtains were left open and the criss-crossed sticky tape was removed from the windows. This tape was similar to masking tape and was supposed to keep the glass in one piece, or at least in large pieces, in the event of the windows being blown in or out by a bomb blast.

The victory celebrations in May 1945 were widely reported in the press. One such report stated that: *In Lee there were many street parties in Pier Street and High Street, the parties were organised by Mr Waterworth (the manager of Lee Tower cinema) and Mr Reid — each child given a flag, two oranges and a shilling.*

Through the efforts of military and civilian personnel, the Service establishments did a great deal for youngsters both in the latter part of the War and afterwards. In December 1944, a party was held in one of the hangars at Fort Grange aerodrome for children of servicemen and civilian personnel from all of the local military establishments in the area. In June 1945, a Victory party was organised by the combined personnel of HMS Daedalus for 500 local children of mixed ages. The event was held in the ballroom at Lee Tower, where a large spread of food was laid out, even though rationing was still in force and food had not been very plentiful for more than five years. Each child was given a commemorative victory spoon as a memento.

Of course, after the War, things did not get back to normal immediately and it took a long time for many people to rebuild their lives, re-establish their relationships and adjust to a changed world. This is illustrated by the incident in which an RAF prisoner of war returned to his family in Anglesea Road. Shortly after his return, his wife had a baby. Unfortunately, according to the gossip of the time, the baby's arrival was too early by too many months. The wife, who had worked in the bar at Lee Tower, was known to occasionally 'entertain' lonely sailors at home – just a case of the War having an adverse effect upon people's behaviour, resulting in them doing things which they would not normally contemplate. The returning husband proved to be very understanding, the family stayed together, and young Bobby had a baby brother … well, that was half right!

Even some years after the War, local people who had suffered damage and loss during the hostilities were still appreciating the charity and generosity of others, and sometimes such kindness came from unexpected sources. In February 1949, a Swiss Legation attended Lee Tower and gave out gift tokens to 15 Gosport families for two beds, a wardrobe, a table and four chairs each. The furniture had been made by Swiss craftsmen in their spare time and the items were later delivered direct to the homes of the grateful recipients.

21

MIDDLE-AGED SPREAD

After the end of the War, many changes began to take place in Lee-on-the-Solent and a great deal of building work was undertaken. The largest building programme consisted of building temporary accommodation in the form of 'prefabs', some of which were established on the land behind Gosport Road and Brickland Terrace. An article in *The Hampshire Telegraph and Post* of March 1946 noted: *Prefabs come to Lee ... they were completed in less than two hours of arrival on site. The foundations for 40 houses had been prepared, and were situated in Elmore Road. Fifteen men to a gang, 5 on the gantries which lift the sections from the lorries and push them into position on runners to the site, 4 fitting sections together, two putting the finishing touches, two working inside – remaining man is the cook. Quickest time one and a half hours. These aluminium houses are gabled painted green and cream. On this site gas for cooking – similar houses on another site will be all electric. Kitchen fitted with cooker refrigerator and deep sink.*

One particular feature commented upon by the local residents when they saw the prefabs being delivered was that they had fridges. Not many houses at that time would have had a fridge, especially in Elmore. For most housewives, the only way to keep food cool was by placing it near the fine wire mesh that formed a small window on the outside wall in the pantry. Keeping food cool was always a problem and, if there had been a thunderstorm in the summer, it would be quite common to have scones (when the other ingredients were available) because the milk would have curdled. The scones were a means of using that milk.

With the roads that were built with them, the prefabs extended Elmore Avenue so that it joined up with Anglesea Road. Before and during the War, the generally overgrown gaps between the houses in Elmore were known as 'greens'. After the War, these began to be built upon and bungalows and houses soon filled in the gaps in Gosport Road, Wootton Road and the bottom of Raynes Road, until eventually all the 'greens' had given way to housing.

In November 1946, there was concern that Lee's historic Le Breton farmhouse was under threat from a proposal to widen the road to 60 ft *[18m]*, but fortunately the property was spared.

Le Breton Farmhouse, Manor Way, 1893

A far more alarming proposal, as far as local residents were concerned, arose in 1948 when British post-War urban planner Max Lock (1909-1988) presented his analysis and report on the development of Portsmouth and South East Hampshire which had been commissioned jointly by the Hampshire County Council and the Portsmouth City Council. In it, he advocated that the population of Lee-on-the-Solent should be allowed to increase from 4,000 to 11,000 by accommodating people from Portsmouth, and that the military should be required to surrender land to enable such expansion to proceed. In particular he wrote that *the restricting influences of the belt of Crown lands which encircle Gosport should be relieved. The War Department should relinquish 285 acres of land between Alverstoke and Lee-on-the-Solent, now rarely, if ever, used by them. The loss will have a negligible effect on the Services concerned.* Effectively Lee-on-the-Solent was to replace Leigh Park in becoming Portsmouth's overspill. This proposal was, of course, never adopted and the 1959 *Hampshire Development Plan for Gosport* not only supported the retention of the character of Lee as a small holiday resort, but also recommended the provision of a Green Belt between it and the built-up area of Gosport. We have already seen, in Chapter 15, that the general 'no housing' policy for this area continues to be maintained to this day by Gosport Borough Council's refusal to countenance the use of the Browndown Camp site for residential development.

In December 1950, there was a suggestion that the proposed development of 275 acres at Lee would be reduced to a 40-acre area. However, in the following February, Hampshire County Council granted permission for housing development on 274 acres to the north of Lee. Other new estates followed, by which the whole area covered by the developed town increased most significantly. In 1976-1977, a large housing development programme was completed around Fell Drive. In October 1983, permission was granted to Wilcon Homes to build 176 new homes on land between Broom Way on the west and Common Barn Lane on the east. All of the roads on this estate were named after birds. Later further development occurred, pushing the limits of the residential area beyond the location of the Wyvern public house. In the early years of the new century 1,050 houses were built on land on the east side of Common Barn Lane. The town has indeed grown considerably over the years, although not perhaps in the way that the Robinson family would ever have envisaged.

22
DEVIATING FROM THE STRAIGHT AND NARROW

I n its edition of Saturday 19 May 1894, *The Hampshire Telegraph* painted this somewhat lyrical picture of life in Lee-on-the-Solent at that time: *The residents ... not very numerous at present, but select – slightly invert the Christian maxim by being of the world, but not in it. About them they will find such surroundings of modern civilisation as a pier, an hotel, with a lawn-tennis ground and a comfortable assembly-room attached, and a bathing machine: and withal they are out of the busy world, and, with the sea on one side and the rural beauties of nature on the other, dwell in a lotus-land of calm delight. Daisies and buttercups are strewn around, the lark sings merrily on high in the air, and the sweet, rich notes of the cuckoo and the nightingale are not wanting to complete the attraction.*

In reality Lee-on-the-Solent like any other place – never was, nor would be, such a Utopia – and there are many reported cases down the years reflecting the ever-changing social issues. A selection of four slightly unusual cases reported in the newspapers during the early years of the town makes interesting reading:

November 1890 – George Stanley (46), a Gosport labourer, set fire to a stack of straw and a stack of hay, the property of John Henry Drewitt of Swaggs Farm, Lee. He pleaded guilty at Winchester Assizes the following month. The prosecution said that several times Stanley had asked people for work and, as he could not get any, he vowed that he was not going to walk the roads any longer. The judge, Mr Justice Grantham, said that it was the act of "a base character towards a man who had done him no harm", and sentenced Stanley to eighteen months' hard labour.

August 1922 – A bizarre case occurred of a man being branded in his sleep. Ernest Victor Moggs, a barman at the Victoria Hotel (now The Bun Penny), suffered three large burns to his left arm while he slept. John Aherne (18) from County Meath was employed at the hotel as a porter and was charged with inflicting grievous bodily harm by the use of "a caustic stick". It was alleged that Aherne, who admitted to being a Sinn Fein supporter, told Moggs that as he had Sinn Fein marks on his body he was liable to shot at any moment. So unnerved was Moggs that he was too ill to appear in Court.

October 1924 – Mrs Kathleen Herbert of Shute Farm was killed by the accidental firing of a rifle held by her son, Frederick Ashton Herbert, a private in the Hampshire Territorials. He had been shooting at Browndown ranges and later returned home, where he picked up his rifle with the intention of showing his parents how it was used. While placing a cartridge in the weapon it accidentally went off, shooting his mother through the chest.

April 1926 – A safe containing important official documents was reported missing from the RAF aerodrome. A large-scale search was undertaken and, working on "certain information conveyed to the police", it was recovered a couple of days later in some furze about a mile away from the base. The safe was intact, but it was clear that there had been attempts to open it. Investigations into the disappearance had been hampered by the fact that many RAF men were on leave for the Easter holidays and it was decided to recall them.

During the Second World War, contrary to popular myth, there was no noticeable reduction in the volume of crime, although by today's standards, many of the things that people were charged with – and for which they had to appear before the magistrates – do not appear at all serious. In fact some cases even seem quite trivial, as this selection of annotations from press reports of the time illustrate:

June 1940 – Roger Taylor (20) of Elmore Road, Ernest Stacey (19) of Elmore Avenue, Alf Easen (16) and Norman Haynes of Seymour Road were charged with playing pitch and toss near Elmore Road, each told to pay 4s [£8.75] costs.

October 1943 – Mrs Ada Tatham of Belle Vue Hotel, Marine Parade East, was fined £1 *[£36]* with 17s *[£30]* costs for using binoculars in a regulated area. (Was she a spy or merely a Peeping Thomasina?)

September 1941 – Diana Lloyd Owen of Canford, Manor Way, was fined 5s *[£10]* for riding her bicycle on the footpath in Marine Parade and Ellie Millard of 6 Pier Street was fined 7s 6d *[£15]* for keeping a dog without a licence.

March 1940 – Maud Bryant of 4 Brickland Cottages was charged with stealing potatoes to the value of 2s *[£4.40]*, the property of her employers, C H House and Sons of Court Barn, Lee-on-the-Solent. She pleaded guilty and was bound over for six months.

July 1943 – Gosport hay theft – two 14 year old boys took some hay from a field at Common Barn Lane, Lee. The owner, Col M House of Crofton Manor, caught them and they were charged with theft. Col House said he had taken the action because he had suffered much damage to hay and straw ricks and fodder – the case was considered proven but dismissed: costs 7s 6d *[£13.60]* each.

It does seem that much police time was taken up with cases that involved people cycling without lights. The standard fine during the War appears to have been 5s *[£9]* for no front light, plus 5s *[£9]* for no rear light. Later the fine went up to 10s *[£18]* per light. The air-raid wardens were equally busy catching people for contravening blackout regulations:- there were numerous cases placed before the magistrates, and the fine for this could be up to £1 *[£36]*.

There were, of course, other more serious matters to concern the police during the War. For example, in February 1940, Walter Harman of Seymour Road received a sentence of three months for insulting behaviour to three women. Later in the year, a gunner (22) was charged with grave offences against two little girls in an air-raid shelter at Lee-on-the-Solent Recreation Ground. On 9 September 1940, he was fined £2 *[£87]*. Perhaps the descriptions used in these two reports were effectively euphemisms for indecent exposure. In December 1943, Charles Herbert Greenwood (33) of 4 Marine Court

Mansions was sent for trial on a charge of assaulting Hazel Doreen Nevill (17) of Titchfield and stealing the contents of her handbag, being £2 [£74]. She had accepted a lift in his car, but he did not stop at her destination and struck her on the head with a cycle lamp before she managed to make her escape.

Even very serious incidents still occurred. The following report appeared in *The Hampshire Telegraph and Post* on 2 May 1941 under the headline: *Poignant Diary Passages – Lee Murder Charge.*

An allegation that "a good time for herself was of more importance to her than anything else" was made in a diary, extracts from which were read at Gosport Police Court on Wednesday, when Donald Jack Chilvers (30) a fitter was accused of murdering his wife.

The diary also describes how, after being told they were going to pictures, he saw his wife and her woman friend with two naval men at a dance. She refused him a dance and told him not to spoil her evening.

Chilvers, since December 14th last had lived with his wife and one of his three children at Sunnyside, Petrie Road, Lee-on-the-Solent. His wife Sybil Ann Chilvers (25) was found stabbed to the heart in the downstairs front room in the early hours of March 26th. She was a handsome blonde and was formerly beauty queen of Norwich.

The prosecution stated that Chilvers lived at Sunnyside, Petrie Road. Upstairs were a Mr and Mrs Chambers. Mrs Chambers and Mrs Chilvers were in the habit of going out together. On Tuesday 25th they went out together telling Chilvers they were going to Gosport to the pictures. In fact they went to a dance, and Chilvers saw them at the dance in the company with two petty officers. This upset him and he returned home with Mrs Chambers and his wife having met them in the street.

At five minutes to four in the morning Chilvers phoned the police and said "Send the ambulance something terrible has happened at Sunnyside". When the police officer arrived and questioned him…he said "You will see if you go in there" (pointing to the living room). Mrs. Chilvers was lying dead on the mat – He told the police he had killed her and the weapon he had stabbed her with was on the mantelpiece. On the mantelpiece was a blood-stained knife. Extracts from his diary were read. She (his wife) said she was going to the pictures. I decided to go out myself and went to a dance to cheer myself up. About 9.30 Sybil and Pearl (Mrs Chambers) came in with two naval fellows. Once again she lied to me. I asked her for a dance. She refused me and told me not to spoil her evening. I went home and waited for the girls to come home; they did not come and I went out to meet them. They were with two naval fellows. I tried to talk to Sybil but she shouted me down ...

He also wrote: Sybil has hurt me in every possible way that a woman can hurt a man ... I would have forgiven Sybil for everything, but Sybil would not have it that way. A good time for herself was of more importance to her than anything else. I cannot bear to think of somebody else making love to her. So I have killed her. Only God, Sybil and myself know what has happened between us young people. God, he does not talk; Sybil is dead, and I myself will soon be dead also.

In the item, the newspaper also reports that Chilvers said that there were letters from other men, and he urged the police to find them, but none was found. It is not clear what happened to Chilvers in the end.

In October 1942, an ATS girl was arrested in Lee and charged with murdering her newly born son. A contemporary report stated: *Appearing in her A.T.S. uniform Beatrice Dauphinais (26) believed to be a native of Brighton and of French extraction was at Brighton on Monday remanded on bail until October 7 charged with the murder of the newly born male child on July 7. The girl was arrested at Lee-on-the-Solent where she had been lodging. It is believed that she had been stationed in the Gosport Area.*

A look at some of the local criminal and other reports in newspapers shortly after the War gives an interesting insight into the social issues of that time:

13 January 1949 – A private in the REME was sent for trial accused of breaking into Down Cottage in Manor Way, the home of Sheila Swanston. He had been sleeping in a hut at the swimming pool.

July 1950 – Widow Lily Guy (70) of 'Guysden', Grove Road, took her own life.

June 1951 – A naval airman stationed at HMS Daedalus was fined £4 *[£100]*, £3 *[£76]* and £3 *[£76]*, a total of £10 *[£252]* in respect of three offences of indecent behaviour at Lee on 18 June.

There were also a couple of murders around this time. In one, a barmaid from the Lee Tower bar was killed outside the San Diego Road Post Office in Gosport. In another, a woman who lived at the junction of Angelsea Road in Gosport was murdered while out walking her dog over the warren or 'wild grounds'. The person convicted lived in Station Road in Brockhurst. Interestingly, this incident took place in an area known as 'hangman's hollow', not far from Apple Dumpling Bridge. Unsubstantiated legend has it that this site was where someone had hanged themselves and for many years afterwards the grass there was tended in the shape of a cross.

23

A SIGHT FIT FOR A KING

M any fleet reviews have taken place in the Solent at Spithead and they have generally been carried out to commemorate mobilisation for war, celebration of victory, presentation of colours, coronations and jubilees. Although the first formal Royal Review was conducted by George III in 1773, there had been Royal Fleet reviews as far back as 1346.

The first Royal Review that occurred after the founding of Lee-on-the-Solent was for the Golden Jubilee of Queen Victoria in 1887, when 128 vessels took part. On that occasion, the presence of a Nordenfelt submarine caused considerable interest. Since then there have been a further 19 reviews. The largest, although never advertised, was the Inspection of the D-Day invasion fleet at anchor in May 1944, when 800 vessels ranging from capital ships to landing craft were assembled.

The review carried out on 25 June 1814 was the last to consist solely of sailing ships, all of which were veterans of the Napoleonic Wars. Due to mental infirmity, King George III was unable to attend and so Prince Regent carried out the review. Six years later, in September 1820, George IV held the first Coronation Review and among the ships in that fleet was *HMS Beagle* on which Charles Darwin travelled between 1831 and 1836.

Queen Victoria held 17 fleet reviews, the first of which was in 1842. However, the review for her Diamond Jubilee in 1897, and also the last of her reign in 1899, were carried out by the Prince of Wales, the future Edward VII, because the Queen was too frail to preside.

It was not only gatherings of the British Navy that caused great excitement. In August 1905, the French Northern Squadron arrived at Cowes and it was estimated that about 40,000-50,000 spectators from London alone came south on special trains to witness the event. Reports of the time indicate that about half a million people gathered at different local vantage points and that the beaches at Lee-on-the-Solent and at Stokes Bay were completely full.

In 1937 George VI reviewed the fleet for his Coronation. This is probably best remembered for the radio broadcast in which a BBC radio announcer, Lt Cdr Tommy Woodroffe, was obviously well-inebriated and rambling. A recording of his famous "The fleet's lit up" commentary survives and is available on the internet.

In 1953 Queen Elizabeth II held a Coronation Fleet Review, in 1969 she reviewed the NATO fleet, and in 1977 she reviewed the fleet for her Silver Jubilee.

The most recent review was in 2005 when she conducted the International Fleet Review as a Trafalgar commemoration, during which we were very careful not to offend the French!

24

SAILING BY

Nowadays, in addition to the splendid spectacle of the yachts, Lee-on-the-Solent is a prime location for watching the arrival and departure of cruise liners. Back in the 1930s, 40s and 50s it was the place to be in order to see the great passenger liners in their heyday when they sailed between Southampton and New York, many competing for the Blue Riband (Hayles Trophy). *Queen Mary* won the award in 1936 but in 1937 *Normandie* captured it, then in 1938 *Queen Mary* regained it. *SS United States* was awarded the trophy in 1952 and this was the last time it was competed for.

The great liners of this era that sailed through the Solent include the *Queen Elizabeth*, *Mauretania*, *Isle de France*, *United States*, *Washington* and *Caronia* which, unlike the rest of the Cunard fleet, had her hull painted light green and not the usual Cunard black. She was the first purpose-built cruise ship, but her design had to be changed during construction. She was known as 'the millionaire's yacht' and her maiden voyage from Southampton to New York was on 4 April 1949. In addition to these, there were the P&O liners such as *Himalaya* and *Corfu* on route to Australia or Hong Kong.

The Union Castle Line, well-known for its lavender-painted ships' hulls, ran to a clockwork timetable between Southampton and South Africa. Every Thursday at 4pm a Union Castle Royal Mail ship would leave Southampton bound for Cape Town. At the same time a Union Castle ship would leave Cape Town on its way to Southampton. All of the vessels would have the name of a castle, such as *Stirling Castle* and *Winchester Castle*. The Castle ships would sail past Lee-on-the-Solent just after five o'clock.

In 1961 the P&O ship *SS Canberra* called at Southampton on its voyages to and from Australia, although this service was short-lived due to the advent of travel by jet planes. The wealthy and famous gradually abandoned the leisurely luxury travel of the opulent liners for the then rather exclusive speed and convenience of an aeroplane.

The great ships ceased to run a scheduled service and became cruise liners, and what was once the preserve of the wealthy and famous gradually became affordable for many more people. Now, with the building of larger and larger ships, taking a cruise has become quite commonplace but, of course, not quite so luxurious.

25

ALL WORK AND NO PLAY

From the earliest days the Robinsons did not limit themselves to the business of developing the new resort, but were also prominent in various social aspects of the new community. For example, the Lee-on-the-Solent Amateur Athletics Club had been formed and it had its first meeting on 2 August 1886. The report of its annual meeting at the cricket ground on 15 September 1888 records that Charles Edmund Robinson, Edmund Arthur Robinson (who was also Honorary Secretary of the Club) together with a third brother, Frederick Sydney Robinson, were all members of the Club's committee. After the brass band had played and the various events had been held, the prizes were awarded by Sir John Charles Robinson who, together with Lady Robinson, was given three hearty cheers.

The cricket ground had been laid out within the first few of years of the Robinson family's purchase. Together with some lawn tennis courts, it occupied a six-acre site bounded by Grove Road, Studland Road, Lulworth Road and Russell Road. Clanwilliam Road did not exist in the early days of the development and was only built later when the cricket pitch had ceased to exist. Within a short time, a small pavilion was erected on the site at the Studland Road side. Around the same time, tennis lawns and a bowling green were established in the grounds of the Victoria Hotel.

Charles Robinson also actively promoted sailing in the area, and the first regatta following the family's purchase of the land was held on the waters off Lee by the Royal Portsmouth Corinthian Yacht Club on 15 July 1885. Two omnibuses were laid on from Gosport Hard via Forton and Brockhurst to Lee, and from Gosport Hard via Stoke

Road and Bury Road to Lee, to bring in spectators. Charles Robinson personally donated one hundred guineas *[£9,300]* to the prize fund.

A swimming club was established in 1927, some four years before construction work began on the seafront swimming pool. The first Club President was Dr G Walter Loughborough MRCS, LRCP, a prominent local physician and surgeon who was also a keen golfer and member of the Lee Ratepayers' Association. He took a particular interest in 'healthy pursuits' and was enthusiastic about the natural qualities of Lee-on-the-Solent, as can be seen from part of the introduction he wrote to the 1927 Official Town Guide: *The climate of Lee is mild but bracing sea breezes in summer prevent extreme heat, while in winter the temperature is seldom cold. The soil is gravel, the water supply excellent. The general health is very good and it is an excellent place for children, especially in the spring and summer months. The difference in the general health and appearance of many children coming here from London and other large towns is most marked, even after only a few weeks stay. It is an ideal spot for convalescing after illness.*

A couple of years later, in 1929, the Lee-on-the-Solent Dramatic Society performed its first production, *Hay Fever* by Noel Coward, at the RAF Station.

While many varied associations and clubs were established, some fell by the wayside but here are a few examples of the some that still exist today:

Angling

For many years the local fishermen kept their boats and equipment on the foreshore under the cliffs. This arrangement was by no means secure either from the weather or from theft or vandalism. As already mentioned, it was necessary to undertake a series of coastal protection measures, which were completed in the early 1960s, to combat the problems of cliff erosion. As part of this work, the local fishermen had to move their boats and they began to consider acquiring some land upon which they could store their craft and equipment. Following discussions and meetings, the Elmore Angling Club was established in August 1959 and was able to rent from the local authority a stretch of the cliff at Elmore.

It was not long before competitions and matches were organised through Club meetings held at various locations around the town. Later, the Club managed to raise sufficient funds to secure the use of a wooden hut as a meeting place before commencing building works on a new clubhouse in April 1978, which finally opened in December of the following year.

Golf

The Lee-on-the-Solent Golf Club was formed at a meeting of 33 men (one of whom was Mr J Cruickshank of Edinburgh House School, see Chapter 9) and seven women in the Victoria Hotel on 28 February 1905. Sir John Charles Robinson was elected as President and J Ramsay became the first Captain. On Chark Common land was leased, a clubhouse erected at a cost of £500 [£44,000] and an 18-hole course was established which opened later that year on 8 November. In 1907, a Ladies section was formed.

A guide book of 1910 records the 18-hole green fees of the time:-

Winter season	1s [£4] for ladies	1s.6d. [£6] for men
Summer season	1s.6d [£6] for ladies	2s.6d [£10] for men
Weekly tariff	6s [£25] for ladies	10s.6d [£44] for men

During the Second World War, an area covering four holes on the course was given over to the growing of crops.

In 1962 the Club was able to purchase the land and a new clubhouse was built seven years later. This was replaced by the present building in 1997.

Sailing

The Lee-on-the-Solent Sailing Club was established in 1907 with Col Sloan-Stanley, Deputy Lord Lieutenant of Hampshire, as the first Commodore. A wooden hut was built by six founder members near the pier and railway station to serve as a clubhouse and six two-day regattas were held annually between 1908 and the outbreak of the Great War.

One Club member erected a new boathouse with refreshment and changing facilities towards the western end of Marine Parade in 1938 but, perhaps because of the slightly distant location, this and its nearby moorings did not prove particularly popular. During the Second World War a lease was granted to the Club on land at Elmore (the site of the present Signals Station) where a compound and two wooden huts were established.

Following the end of the War, the Club wanted to establish a proper clubhouse to cater for the needs of the growing membership and, in 1951, was able to purchase its present premises in Marine Parade East. After much work, the new clubhouse opened in December 1954. Since that time, enhancements have been made to provide a new gallery and bar.

On the Club's other site, a new Signals Station building was constructed in the early 1950s and further land was acquired to form three compounds which now have 146 berths.

In 2012 the Club announced proposals for redevelopment of the clubhouse site involving the demolition of the existing building and the construction of a new one consisting of flats at one end and a new clubhouse at the other.

Tennis

In the very early days of the development of the town, public tennis lawns were established on part of the cricket pitch site (see above) and, when these were closed, two grass courts were laid out on the cliff top immediately west of the pier, near the junction of Marine Parade West and Milvil Road.

In 1908, the Lee-on-the-Solent Lawn Tennis Club was established and used these facilities but, in 1919, a new purpose-built clubhouse with grass courts was developed on the western side of Manor Way. The old public courts at the seafront became a putting green. The grass courts at the new premises were later changed to clay and, in the 1930s, the Club became one of the first in the area to provide squash courts.

In 1978 a major refurbishment was undertaken, an extension constructed and the courts were brought up to top modern standards. Now, under the name of Lee-on-the-Solent Tennis, Squash and Fitness Club, the facilities include six all-weather tennis courts, six squash courts, a gymnasium, bar and lounge.

Community Centre

The ever-growing population has often outstripped facilities which have been provided for the use of the community over the years. We have already seen how the Lowry Memorial Hall in the High Street was an early, popular and much-used venue. Each of the three church buildings in Lee have also added halls for use by both congregations and non-church groups alike. With the large numbers of houses built on the developments towards the north end of Lee from the 1970s onwards, it was clear that a new purpose-built community centre was needed.

In 1977 the Lee United Action Group was formed with the aim of securing a site upon which a new centre could be established. Fortunately Col House had donated land in Twyford Drive for the use of the community and the Group managed to negotiate grants from Hampshire County Council and Gosport Borough Council conditional upon the community matching that funding. A huge fund-raising programme organised by the Group eventually secured sufficient finance to enable construction works on the new community centre to begin in August 1981. This was completed early the following year and the centre opened on 29 March 1982.

Just three years later it was already apparent that the building was unable to cater for all those wishing to use its facilities, so an extension was added. Outside enhancements were also made and the car park was enlarged to provide 92 spaces.

By 1992 membership had grown to 1,700 and another extension was completed in July 1993 and further refurbishment has been undertaken since then.

Hovercraft Museum

As mentioned in Chapter 16, Lee-on-the-Solent was closely connected with the development of hovercraft and in 1971 the Hovercraft Society was founded. In April 1986 a private individual was able to acquire the last surviving SRN5, which was donated at no cost by Hovertravel at a time when its fleet was being replaced with newer models. Later, when Hovermarine International went into liquidation, another craft became available and a group of enthusiasts set up a charitable trust in 1988 to manage both craft and to build a collection, archive and library which would be incorporated into a museum of hovercraft. The Museum took a site on the airfield near the waterfront just opposite the main slipway.

On 16 December 1989, the 80ft *[24m]*-long hovercraft BH7 returned to Daedalus. Saved from the scrap yard, but with the engines already removed, it was necessary to tow the vessel across the Solent from East Cowes. Air blowers mounted on a lorry were then attached to the craft to enable it to hover so that it could then be pulled up the slipway for restoration at Lee. A little later, in 1994, a cross Channel hovercraft, capable of carrying 37 cars, was towed round from Dover to Lee.

The Museum is open to the public for a few days each year and runs a popular annual Hovershow. Staffed entirely by volunteers, it now has 60 hovercraft and an extensive library and archive and is the only museum of hovercraft in the world.

Lee Residents' Association (LoSRA)

Local public feeling was stirred up when, late in 1972, Michael Leopold discovered that developers wanted to fill in Elmore Lake with a view to building houses on the site. He and a number of others formed a steering committee the following February to resist the proposal and, through this, the Lee-on-Solent Residents' Association came into being. The proposal was indeed defeated and the Association quickly grew in membership and strength. In November 2004 it merged with Vision4Lee which had been formed in 2004 for the purpose of focusing on ways in which the economy of the town could be enhanced in order to make it a better place in which to live.

While the primary aim has always been to represent the needs and interests of local residents, the scope of the Association's role has been extended. It now keeps its membership of over 1,000 fully up to date on local issues and proposals, provides a platform for local views, helps enhance open spaces and holds various meetings and events throughout the year for the benefit of the community.

Women's Institute

The inaugural meeting of the Lee-on-the-Solent Women's Institute was held on 29 April 1927 when Lady Wells VCO delivered an address to about 30 members. On that occasion the first officers were appointed: Mrs Campbell Perkins (President), Mrs Metcalfe (Vice-President), Mrs Bovill (Secretary) and Mrs Webb (Treasurer) and from its inception the branch proved to be very popular. By October of that year, membership had already risen to 65 and by February 1930 it had doubled once again to 130.

An early WI production of 'School for Scandal' held in Miss LaMotte's garden at Court End, Lee-on-the-Solent

The Lowry Hut in the High Street became the home of the Institute's evening meetings and, when the main room of the hut was taken over as a services canteen during the Second World War, the branch decamped to the smaller hall within the building. Unfortunately the early years of the War were not a good time for the branch, which saw its activities greatly curtailed and its membership drop to about 30 by June 1942. Yet, due to the zeal and hard work of Mrs Furze, who had been elected Secretary at that time, the number of members began to rise until it eventually became the largest branch in the whole of Hampshire. At this time the provision of tea was becoming a problem and this was only solved by the introduction of a contribution levy from each member of 1d *[15p]* a cup.

During the War years, the branch was able to maintain morale by holding a number of birthday parties and garden parties. Fundraising for urgent causes was also a major feature and sometimes required considerable ingenuity. On one occasion, when lemons had all but disappeared due to wartime restrictions, one was somehow produced by a member, Miss Brown. It formed the prize in a penny raffle in which it alone realised 5s 8d *[£9.75]*. 1944 was a difficult year locally, with Lee being crowded with servicemen and vehicles being made

Another early WI amateur dramatic production staged in Miss LaMotte's
Garden at Court End, Lee-on-the-Solent.
Miss LaMotte is standing extreme right

ready for the D-Day assault. Arrangements had been made at this time for the birthday party to be held at the Lowry Hut as usual, but at the last minute it was discovered that, due to wear and tear at the hands of great numbers of servicemen, there was a not a single serviceable chair available in the building and it was impossible to use the facility. The minister of the Methodist Church very kindly came to rescue just in time and offered the use of his church hall. The party was quickly relocated and proved to be a great success. For the next few weeks, the meetings were held at the church hall on Tuesday afternoons before reverting to the Lowry Hut in November 1944. By this time there were 90 members on the books, some of whom had been involved earlier in the year with the scheme of distributing strawberries to some of the service personnel embarking for D-Day.

With the end of hostilities, the branch was able to expand its activities, membership steadily increased and drama once again became an important factor, encouraging lively interest. Performances including comedy, pantomime, rehearsed charades, miming and even light opera were given to Naval Friendly Wives, Sisterhood, Mothers' Union and other organisations. On these occasions, the considerable wardrobe would all be produced by the industry of the members themselves.

With the eventual closure of the Lowry Hut, meetings were held in the Methodist Church from 1979 before moving to the Community Centre in 1990, where the branch still meets on the last Thursday of each month. However the glory days are now sadly gone and, whereas membership stood at about 40 a couple of years ago, it is down to 23 at the time of writing. Nevertheless, the spirit remains and the ladies continue to enjoy a variety of meetings, functions and outings.

A day at the races —
the members of the WI have moved on from amateur dramatics

Working Men's Club

A group of eight men (Messrs W Morris, G Over, F Marlow, C Punter, J Malt, J Williams, T Betteridge and C Towner) came together in the summer of 1900 to form the Lee-on-the-Solent Working Men's Club. Mr W Morris was appointed President, a role in which he continued for the following 32 years, and Mr C Towner took on the post of Secretary. The Club was registered on 5 July that year and became affiliated to the CIU on 11 August 1900. Early meetings and functions were held above the lock-up garage and workshop premises of W J Young, builders, near the primary school at Elmore, but it was not long before the Club was looking to move its activities to better premises. Mr Frederick Flower (see Chapter 8) had been an early prominent member and, largely through his efforts, the Club was able to use part of Flower Buildings on Marine Parade.

In 1920 the Club moved again to its present location in the High Street. This was then a prefabricated asbestos hut, which was later clad in corrugated sheeting. The new clubhouse incorporated this older building as part of the club facilities until the old hut was demolished in August 1988 and replaced shortly afterwards by an extension, which now houses the games room. The new extension was constructed by Molson UK Ltd and completed on 10 November 1988.

During the early years, the Club was very much a male-dominated body, although there was one small room available which women and children were allowed to enter, but beyond which they were forbidden to proceed. While this apparent prejudice might seem difficult to understand now it was, of course, very common in those times and it certainly did not seem to affect the popularity of the Club. For example, the annual accounts for the year ending 31 December 1924 show that the year's takings on bar sales alone amounted to £2,645 15s 1d [£118,000]. In those same accounts the full-time Steward's annual salary appears as £173 [£7,700].

Whilst the Club continues its long history, its heyday is now, sadly, long gone. Membership peaked at around 1,400 in the 1980s but, some 30 years on, now stands at about 700 and, in common with many other local clubs and bodies, it is the younger generation who are not seeking membership in the numbers they once did. Although perhaps being of some cold comfort, the changing fortunes of the Club are not unique and whereas the number of Working Men's Clubs nationally stood at a high of about 4,000 in the 1980s, that figure has since fallen by half.

26

I'M A CELEBRITY – I LIKE IT HERE!

While Lee-on-the-Solent may not have fulfilled the original aspirations of the Robinson family and the early developers it has, over the years, seen occasional visits by famous names.

It has already been noted in Chapter 15 that Queen Victoria, Prince Albert and the Prince of Wales landed at Stokes Bay and visited the encampment at Browndown on 23 August 1856.

In 1898, a prominent Victorian villa was built at the extreme western end of the seafront where Marine Parade turns inland and becomes Stubbington Lane. The property was originally called 'Beachcroft' and was used by the tea and grocery magnate, Sir Thomas Lipton, as a base from which he could operate while indulging his passion for sailing on the Solent. It was incorporated into the military base in the 1930s, renamed 'Ross House', and occupied by successive captains of the base before being demolished in 2000 and replaced by an apartment block. A story exists concerning Lipton's stays at the property. He was a self-made millionaire from relatively humble working-class stock, and not a natural member of the British upper class. He was obsessed with yachting and yacht racing and desperately wanted to join the Royal Yacht Squadron, but the 'snobbery' of those times meant that he was refused admittance for many years. The story alleges that the turret on this house lined up directly with the start line used in the races of Cowes Week. Every time they used to fire the cannon to start a race, he would fire his own from the house. This 'double firing' was interpreted by those yachtsmen taking part that there had been a false start to the race and therefore cause much mayhem. Although the story might be entertaining, it is stressed that no clear evidence can be found in support of it. The authors rather doubt the veracity of it (due to the fact that it would take almost 30 seconds for the sound to carry from and to the vicinity of Cowes) and suspect that it may be just be an amusing but complete myth.

In 1911, Noel Coward is reputed to have made his theatrical debut in a talent show on the pier. As a schoolboy, he frequently spent holidays at a house (since demolished) at Meon, south of Titchfield.

During the Great War, the King of Belgium, Albert I, and his consort, Elisabeth of Bavaria, flew over Lee-on-the-Solent, landed at the pier and made a short visit to the town.

Vivian R Malet was born in Lee in September 1927. He emigrated to the United States in the 1950s, changed his name to Arthur Malet and became an actor. Although not widely known or recognised, he enjoyed a long, varied and prolific career coming to prominence in 1960s films, often playing characters much older than his real age, such as Mr Dawes Jr in *Mary Poppins*. Among a very long list of film and television credits, he appeared in the films *In the Heat of the Night, Halloween,* and *Young Frankenstein* as well as in television episodes of *The Alfred Hitchcock Hour, Bewitched, Dallas, Columbo, The Untouchables, The Man from UNCLE, Hawaii Five-O* and *Dr Kildare.*

In 1929 RAF Aircraftsman John Hume Ross, actually an alias for T E Lawrence ('of Arabia'), was detached to Calshot to help with the Schneider Trophy Race of that year and it is understood that his duties sometimes brought him to the slipway at Lee-on-the-Solent.

Gracie Fields is said to have owned and built, in 1935, an Art Deco style property in Milvil Road called 'Shangri-La'. Under that same name it is now a rest home. Once again, however, no clear evidence can be found for this. The legal title of the property does not reveal any reference to her at the time it was first constructed, no accounts seem to exist of her being in the town at any time, and the story should perhaps be viewed with some caution.

In July 1940 King George VI paid a visit to HMS Daedalus and reviewed the personnel.

King George VI inspecting WRNS on his visit to HMS Daedalus in 1940

In 1941-2 both Laurence Olivier and Ralph Richardson trained together, served as pilots in the Fleet Air Arm, and passed through HMS Daedalus. Olivier had just returned from filming *Rebecca* and *Pride & Prejudice* in the USA, both films being released there in April 1940. Serving as a Lieutenant, he never actually saw combat but was involved in a number of crash- and forced-landings from which he emerged unscathed (indeed, Ralph Richardson commented that they probably held the record for the most pranged aircraft at the base). Olivier had, in fact, been at Lee some years earlier in 1932 when he came with Gloria Swanson to film location shots for the feature film *Perfect Understanding*. In the film, which was not a box-office success, the scenes shot at Lee occur after about 20 minutes and last for only about two minutes. They show a newly married couple, played by Olivier and Swanson, boarding a small aeroplane and taking off to the cheers of their friends and well-wishers. The sequence was filmed at the airfield, but contains nothing to indicate to anyone watching the film today that it was actually shot at Lee.

Actor Rupert Davies, who would later become famous for his television portrayal of French detective, *Maigret*, also served at HMS Daedalus during the War.

During the post-War days, when the Lee air shows were staged, famous names such as Norman Wisdom and Dick Emery made guest appearances.

In September 1948 Prince Philip, Duke of Edinburgh, raced his Dragon Class yacht *Bluebottle* in the Solent during Lee's third regatta.

On 2 December 1949, the BBC recorded an edition of the popular radio programme *Any Questions?* at Lee Tower. Question master Freddy Grisewood was joined by panellists John Arlott, Ralph Wightman, Graham Hutton and 'the radio doctor' Dr C Hill. Some 480 free tickets were issued for the occasion.

Queen Elizabeth II visited HMS Daedalus on 21 November 1952 and witnessed a flypast of representative naval aircraft. She returned to the town on 30 July 1956 when she presented the Queen's Colour to the Royal Naval Barracks at HMS Daedalus. During part of that visit she was entertained at 'Old Place', a bungalow at the northern end of Manor Way which was purchased by the Admiralty in 1950 and later sold on by it in 1961.

Actor and radio presenter Wilfred Pickles visited the town in 1961 to record an edition of his popular radio show *Have a Go* at Lee Tower.

Princess Marina, Duchess of Kent, came to Lee on 18 July 1963 in her capacity as Chief Commandant WRNS, to open a new purpose-built accommodation block for female naval ratings.

On 24 June 1980 Princess Anne, who was at that time Chief Commandant of WRNS, visited HMS Daedalus and met many of the WRNS at work there.

Lee-on-the-Solent is the notional setting of the dialogue spoken by Julie Walters in *Her Big Chance*, one of the BBC *Talking Heads* series of monologues by Alan Bennett, first screened on television in April/May 1988.

Singer Ann Shelton attended the D-Day 50-year anniversary celebrations at the airfield in June 1994. Sadly it was to be one of her last appearances before her death shortly afterwards.

In September 1995 Prince Andrew, the Duke of York, visited HMS Daedalus and gave an address at the Fleet Air Arm Reunion.

Browndown Army Camp was the location for the ITV television series *Lads' Army*, followed by a second series named *Bad Lads' Army*, shown between June 2002 and August 2006.

27

WE WILL REMEMBER THEM

Taking only a casual look at the 'lest we forget' memorial of local people who died, it could be very easy to underestimate the impact and pain caused by the deaths of those named.

Those listed on the memorial for the Great War (1914-1918) are:-

Adams, W.H.	Harrison, H.	Odell, R.
Ayling, W.	Hayward, G.	Odell, W.
Bailey, E.	Hayward, W.	Packham, E.F.
Barnard, R.G.	Hewes, W.G.	Pike, D.
Begbie, S.C.H.	Hellyer, J.	Redman, J.
Bird, W.	Judd, W.	Rye, A.
Burridge, H.G.	King, N.M.	Smith, W.
Burch, F.G.	Locke, C.	Stretch, H.
Clark, H.R.	Lowry, A.E.E.	Thick, H.C.
Coffin, E.	Lowry, C.J.P.	Tizard, C.E.
Cook, A.	Lowry, W. H.	Tribbeck, H.
Cook, W.	Luff, P.	Tutt-Harris, W.
Egremont, L.G.	Lukis, L.C.F.	Ward, A.
Foster, A.C.H.	Marchant, T.	Ward, H.V.
Foster, W.J.	Mead, H.C.	Warland, C.
Franklin, T.J.	Mitchell, J.	Wells, A.
Goodall, T.J.	Morris, E.	Wells, M.
Gover, S.H.	Morris, P.J.	Weyman, E.
Halahan, R.C.	Muckett, S.	Wheeler, H.P.
Hallett, R.	New, F.J.	Wise, H.
Harris, C.R.	Newman, C.	Yonge, C.H.
Harrison, G.	Newman, H.J.	

A total of 65 men were lost from a village with a population of less than 300 males of working age, that is almost one in four, which gives some idea of the effect it must have had on the families in the area and the community at large.

The first of 'the many' was **Harry Stretch** (37), a Chief Stoker serving aboard *HM Submarine AE1* who died on 14 September 1914, just six weeks after the declaration of war. The vessel was on loan from the British Navy and was the first submarine to serve in the Royal Australian Navy. She had been in service for barely seven months when, at 7am on 14 September 1914, she left Blanche Bay in Papua New Guinea to go on a routine patrol off Cape Gazelle. When she had not returned by 8pm several ships were sent out to search for her, but no trace was ever found and it is thought that she was probably wrecked on a reef or other submerged object. The full compliment of a commander and two officers together with 32 sailors (including Stretch) lost their lives and, despite further searches, the wreck was never located. Stretch had been awarded the China Medal in 1900 and also held long-service and good conduct awards. He was among the first 100 to volunteer for submarine work while it was still in its infancy. His parents lived at Stubbington for many years and he was brought up there.

The first casualty of actual enemy action named on the memorial was **Reuben George Barnard** (32), a Ship's Steward RN serving on *HMS Hogue* who died on 22 September 1914, eight weeks after the outbreak of hostilities. On this day three Cressy Class Armoured Cruisers, *HMS Aboukir*, *HMS Cressy* and *HMS Hogue* were sunk by U-boats in the North Sea.

The last to fall during hostilities was **George Alfred Hayward** (31), a Stoker 1st class RN serving on *HMS Victory* who died on 2 November 1918, nine days before the signing of the armistice. He lived at Brickfield Cottages in Lee-on-the-Solent and is buried in the Naval Cemetery at Haslar. However, **Thomas Marchant** (18), a signal boy aboard *HMS Emperor of India*, died of his wounds on 21 February 1919. He lived at Hill Head and is buried at the Naval

Cemetery at Haslar. Additionally **Reginald Vile Hallett** (23), a Gunner in the Royal Field Artillery, died of his wounds on 12 March 1919. His family ran the Red Lion public house in Stubbington and he is buried at Crofton Holy Rood Cemetery.

Late in the afternoon on 1 November 1914, Vice-Admiral Maximilian von Spee's Squadron encountered a British Naval Squadron under the command of Sir Christopher Cradock off the southern coast of Chile. They opened fire and hit Cradock's flagship, *HMS Good Hope*, a Drake Class Armoured Cruiser, which sank within half an hour drowning **James Hellyer**, a Leading Stoker RN; **Connie Aubrey Newman** (23), Engine Room Artificer 3rd Class RN, and **John Ellery Tizard** (28), Assistant Paymaster RN, all from this area. *HMS Monmouth*, a Monmouth Class Armoured Cruiser, was also sunk in this engagement which became known as the Battle of Coronel. In all some 1,600 sailors perished, including Sir Christopher Cradock, making it the Royal Navy's worst defeat in more than a hundred years.

Of course it is immediately noticeable that there are three of the fallen who have the same uncommon surname. They are **Auriol Ernest Eric Lowry** (25), Lieutenant Colonel in the West Yorkshire Regiment, died 23 September 1918 and is buried at La Targette British Cemetery in St Vaast, France; **Cyril John Patrick Lowry** (20), Captain in the West Yorkshire Regiment, died 25 March 1918 and commemorated on the Pozieres Memorial, Somme, France, and **William Augustine Harper Lowry** (25), Second Lieutenant in the Indian Army Reserve of Officers, who died on 4 June 1915 and whose name appears on the Helles Memorial, Turkey. These were the only sons of William and Ann Lowry who moved to Lee-on-the-Solent in the very early days. William Snr was a retired tea planter who lived with his wife and their family at Ryde View on Marine Parade East. They later moved to Manor Way. They commemorated their sons in the creation of the Lowry Memorial Hall (See Chapter 10).

There are three other cases of sibling deaths on the memorial. The first is that of **Archibald Courtenay Hayes Foster** (28), Lieutenant in the Hampshire Regiment attached to the King's African

Rifles who died 18 September 1914 and who is commemorated on the Nairobi British and Indian Memorial, Nairobi, Kenya, and his brother, **William John Foster** (30), Lieutenant Commander aboard *HM Submarine E6* who died 26 December 1915 and whose name appears on the Portsmouth Naval Memorial. Both brothers lived at Stubbington.

The second pair of brothers is **Reginald Arthur Odell** (25), Sergeant in the Hampshire Regiment who died 30 June 1916. He was mentioned in dispatches and is commemorated on the Basra Memorial, Iraq, and **William James Odell** (29), Sergeant in the Hampshire Regiment who died 12 March 1918 and is commemorated on the Tehran Memorial, Iraq. Both brothers lived at Hill Head.

Of the third pair of brothers, **Arthur Wells** (40), Private in the Hampshire Regiment died 7 October 1917, is buried at the Agra Cantonment Cemetery, India and is commemorated on the Madras 1914-1918 War Memorial, Chennai, India. He lived at Bricklands Terrace, Gosport Road, Lee-on-the-Solent. His brother was **Matthias Wells** (32), Private in the Hampshire Regiment who died 3 September 1916 and is commemorated on the Thiepval Memorial, Somme, France. He lived at Gosport Road, Lee-on-the-Solent.

Most of those mentioned on the memorial are also remembered on other memorials or buried in "some corner of a foreign field that is forever England", but four of them **(Reginald Vile Hallett, George Henry Harrison, Eric Frank Packham** and **Harold Tribbeck)** are buried at Crofton Holy Rood Cemetery, and two **(George Alfred Hayward** and **Thomas Marchant)** at the Haslar Royal Naval Cemetery. **Charles Ronald Harris** is buried at Ann's Hill Cemetery, **Harold Royston Clark** is buried at Fareham Cemetery and **William Herbert Adams** is buried at St Mary's Churchyard, Hook.

Although no less painful for the families concerned, the list of those killed in the Second World War is, thankfully, much smaller than those who fell in the previous great conflict. However there are two surnames that appear for both World Wars, and two for one family.

Those listed on the memorial for the Second World War (1939-1945) are:-

Browning, G.	Drayson, A.C.	Hunter, D.E.
Buck, W.E.	Evans, C.G.	Nixon, S.D.
Clark, L.T.G.*	Field, V.B.	Philbrick, M.E.
Cook, H.E.*	Fitch, C.	Roberts, C.H.T.
Copland, B.L.	Fitch, J.D.	Smart, W.M.
Dimmick, C.D.	Grout, C.L.A.	Wilkinson, R.A.W.
Dimmick, S.H.	Hawkins, L.H.	

*same name for WWI

The following two names were added to those listed above at a later date:

Bryant, P.

Briggs, D.R.

As already mentioned in Chapter 19, Geoffrey Browning and Cecil Grout died in the raid on HMS Daedalus on 16 August 1940. There were other civilian casualties in the same air-raid:

George William Cripps (30) of Canvey Island, Essex,

Charles Richard Dupree (59) of Marine Parade,

John Edward Darrington (29) of Bedford Street, Gosport,

Henry James (40) of Titchfield,

John Howard Lovell (20) of Buckland, Portsmouth, and

Algernon Ernest Whitear (55) of Titchfield.

Later in the War the following civilians were killed:

Lewis Thomas George Clark (32) of Totton, Home Guard, on 26 March 1941 at the South-Western Tar Distilleries. He is buried in the New Forest Rural District Cemetery,

William George Patmore (46) of Fordingbridge, on 21 June 1943 at the Royal Naval Air Station, Lee-on-the-Solent, and

Rev Douglas Egbert Hunter (60) on 16 May 1944 (see Chapter 19). It is believed that his death was a result of an anti-aircraft shell hitting the Vicarage – one of two examples of death due to 'friendly fire' in Lee-on-the-Solent. The other instance is the case of the ten WRNS who were billeted in a large house in Newton Place (later to become the Mansfield House Blind Home and then a Rest Home) (See Chapter 19).

'Big Tom', the anti-aircraft gun referred to in Chapter 19, must be a prime suspect in these two disastrous occurrences. Lines drawn from its location to each of the fatal sites are within 10 degrees of each other and midway between them lies the line to the centre of the area where the hangars were situated. Additionally, the sites where the shells landed are equidistant from the anti-aircraft gun emplacement. It can be seen that 'friendly fire' is not a new phenomenon.

The remaining 16 military casualties of the Second World War named on the memorial are divided more or less equally between the three armed services.

The first casualty was **William Edward Buck** (24), a Driver with the Royal Army Service Corps. He died on 20 March 1940 during the fighting in Palestine, when it was known as the British Mandate of Palestine, and is buried in the Ramleh War Cemetery.

The first casualty on the memorial to be killed in Europe was **Sidney Harry Dimmick** (21), a Driver in the Royal Engineers who died on 28 May 1940 at Dunkirk. He is buried in Dunkirk Town Cemetery.

In the December of the same year there were two further casualties:

Albert Charles Drayson (21), Able Seaman RN of Lee-on-the-Solent, who died on 14 December 1940. He was aboard the French torpedo boat, *Branlebas* (which the British had captured off Portsmouth on 3 July 1940) when it foundered in a storm off Dartmouth, and

Charles Gentry Evans (39), CPO RN of Gosport, who died on 17 December 1940. He was aboard *HMS Acheron* when she struck a mine and sank off the Isle of Wight.

Both names are also commemorated on the Portsmouth Naval Memorial.

Remarkably, during 1941 and the first half of 1942, although there was one civilian killed as a result of enemy action in Lee-on-the-Solent, no families received the dreaded telegram telling them of the loss of a loved one in the service of their country.

Two members of the same family lost their lives in the conflict: **Cyril Iggo Fitch** (24), Engine Room Artificer 3rd Class aboard *HMS Welshman* (an Abdiel class minelayer), died 1 February 1943 when she was sunk by a U-boat east of Tobruk; he was mentioned in dispatches and is commemorated on the Chatham Naval Memorial, and **Jack Dunning Fitch** (27), Flight Sergeant in the RAF, died 27 December 1942 and is commemorated on the Runnymede Memorial, Surrey. The family lived at Victoria Square, Lee-on-the-Solent.

Two local servicemen died on the same day on 16 July 1943: **Norman Edwin Philbrick** (22), Sergeant in the Royal Air Force Volunteer Reserve of Calne, Wilshire, died in the defence of Malta and is remembered on the Memorial there, and **Roy Albert Wilfred Wilkinson**, Air Gunner, Sergeant RAF, who is buried in the Milan War Cemetery.

The last fatality of a local serviceman was recorded as early as two years before the end of the war. He was **Victor Bowring Field**, Flying Officer RAF, who died on 20 June 1943. He is recorded on the Alamein Memorial. He is also the only officer on the Lee-on-the-Solent War Memorial for the Second World War, the rest of the names being made up of NCOs and other ranks and civilians.

28

AND HERE'S TO YOU, MR ROBINSON

In approaching the end of our account, it might be useful to examine how the original vision for Lee-on-the-Solent, as held by John Robinson and his two sons, became shaped, forged and eventually transformed by events and influences over the last 130 years before finally emerging as the town we know today.

Two years before the arrival of the Robinson family, the 1881 census was carried out. The area which is now Lee-on-the-Solent was classified as being in the Civil Parish of Titchfield, in the Ecclesiastical Parish Crofton Holy Rood and in the Rural Sanitary District of Fareham. The census shows that there were 31 civilian dwellings and a military camp. In total there were 159 residents comprising 74 civilian males over the age of 12, 15 males under the age of 12, 46 females over the age of 12 and 24 females under the age of 12. All of the local inhabitants were effectively involved with agriculture which supported the whole population. This was very much in keeping with what Sir John Robinson commented upon in a speech he made on 31 May 1894, on the opening of the railway branch line, when he recalled that ten years previously ... *the place was nothing but a lone, outlying farm by the sea-side, tenanted only by sheep, cows and pigs and a few rustics devoted in bringing up the animals.*

Henry Drewitt farmed the 590 acres which comprised Melville Farm and employed 30 men and boys. Charles Whettam, farmer, employed 16 men and four boys at Court Barn Farm, which consisted of 415 acres. At the 400-acre Shoot Farm, William H Smith employed 11 men and six boys. At Swaggs Farm, which was somewhat smaller at 62 acres, farmer Nathanial Ellison employed two men. This means that there were 69 men and boys employed in agriculture, mainly as agricultural labourers, together with three shepherds.

Court Barn Farm, circa 1890s

The workers' dwellings were mostly scattered throughout the area, but there was a collection of four dwellings at Butts Cross. This was situated at the northern end of the present Manor Way. On plans of the area from around this time there is residence called Butts Cross Cottage at the top end of Manor Way, on the left, near where the gates of the airfield are now located.

A house at Lee Farm was occupied by a gardener and family. Later census returns show this as Lee Britten Farm. Two houses that were listed at Middle Lee were occupied by a carter and agricultural labourers and their families, probably situated near the junction of the present High Street and Manor Way. Two dwellings which were occupied by a shepherd and an agricultural labourer at Lower Lee may have been situated near the Elmore end of Lee-on-the-Solent, at the southern end of Common Barn Lane. Another shepherd lived at Common Barn.

Although there had been no camp on the site in 1856, by the time of the 1881 census, some 25 years later, a permanent Royal Marines camp had been built at Browndown. Stationed at the camp there were 55 personnel (including families) consisting of a commanding officer, a Colour Sergeant with his family, a Sergeant together with his wife and 37 Privates and other NCOs. Also there was a Government Storekeeper and his family living at the 'Gun Cotton' Fort, (possibly Browndown Battery) and a Lance Corporal as Caretaker of the Rifle Range living with his family at the 'Musketry Hut'.

The 1891 census gives a picture of how, within a few years of the establishment of Lee-on-the-Solent, there were the beginnings of a move away from agriculture as the primary source of employment in the area. Although there had been an increase of just over 50 percent in the number of civilian dwellings to 51, the civilian population had almost doubled to just over 250 with 99 civilian males over the age of 12 and 21 under the age of 12 together with 93 females over the age of 12 and 38 under the age of 12. The number of men and boys employed in agriculture was now 48. Thus the percentage of those employed in agriculture had fallen from over 90 percent to just under 50 percent in just one decade, with men now being employed in roles such as bus-drivers, bakers, grocers, house-painters, brick makers (these lived in Brickland Terrace), engineers, railway porters, and postmen.

The 1891 census also shows that at Browndown camp there were two officers, a Colour Sergeant with his family, a Corporal with his family, 73 Privates and other NCOs and another officer with his wife and family at the 'Musketry Hut'. The military personnel had almost doubled from 40 to 76, much in line with the local population, and with so many virile young men, many in their late teens and twenties, it must have been a case of 'lock up your daughters'. That is unless the young soldiers were enticed into Gosport by its reputation that preceded it, and which was enshrined in a ballad from the Napoleonic wars, which L F W White refers to in his *Story of Gosport*. The ballad is sung to the tune of *A Cobbler There Was*, and the last verse runs as follows:

The want of fine buildings, and grand colonnades,

Is made up by fine women, dear, good-humoured jades;

Though these lasses of pleasure, take black, fair or brown,

Scarce amount to ten thousand in all Gosport town.

Derry down etc.

In an early plan of the estate it is interesting to see that the area at the centre of the triangle formed by the present-day Gosport Road, Elmore Road and Cambridge Road was set aside as 'Stabling'. Perhaps it was envisaged that this would be the proposed location where the horses for the carriages of the wealthy residents of Lee-on-the-Solent would be kept. However within a year or so, in 1886, Karl Benz had constructed the first petrol-driven car and in 1893 Henry Ford began to produce automobiles. This may have marked the first departure from the sedate vision which John Robinson may have had for the estate of wealthy inhabitants travelling in their horse-drawn carriages. It is most likely that it was those very people who would be the first to adopt the new and somewhat less genteel mode of transport.

The last decade of the nineteenth century saw further dramatic changes. Although the second Boer War (1899-1902) occurred just after the 'birth' of Lee-on-the-Solent, it did not have any major impact on the local population and, by the time of the 1901 census, the number of civilian dwellings had grown by over two and a half times to 136. The civilian population had increased by a similar factor and stood at 677 with 255 males over 12 and 87 under 12 (although 44 of these were pupils at the Edinburgh House School) and 255 females over 12 and 80 under 12.

That census shows that there had been a slight resurgence of those employed in agriculture. Some 60 men and boys were employed on the land, which was still only about a quarter of the male working population; however, only 23 (just under one in ten) were employed in the building trade and this was 16 years into the development of Lee. Nevertheless, the number of well-to-do inhabitants settling in

Lee-on-the-Solent was gradually increasing. For example, Edmund Arthur Robinson had taken up residence at 'Melrose' on the corner of Milvil Road and Marine Parade West and nearby was 'Ryde View' which had been bought by William Lowry (47) a retired tea-planter. He had moved in with his wife, three sons, a daughter and four domestic servants. Domestic service was providing employment for quite a number of female local residents in some of the larger houses.

Although the Browndown camp was still there, the number of personnel had been reduced to an officer in charge, a Colour Sergeant and his family, a Sergeant with his family and 14 Privates and other NCOs – a mere 20 percent of what it had been just ten years previously, and the admonition to 'lock up your daughters' no longer held sway – also a certain kind of business in Gosport would have been much less brisk.

Ten years later, the 1911 census recorded the total population of Lee-on-the-Solent as 1,070 (257 males over 18 and 234 under 18 and 358 females over 18 and 221 under 18) occupying 203 dwellings (a century later, in 2011, the population was recorded as 7,224). While the old farms were still present and a small percentage of the population was still employed in agriculture, there had been a massive rise in the number of other occupations, particularly in the building trade (bricklayers, general labourers, decorators, and carpenters) and in shopkeepers (drapers, bakers, butchers). A large number of people listed their occupations as chauffeurs, domestic gardeners and retired army or naval personnel. Additionally many people gave either "private means" or "none" in answer to the occupation enquiry. Some of the more unusual occupations shown include professional golfer, drink manufacturer, shoe-black, artist, and golf-club maker. At Elmore a number of people described their occupation as "scavenger". As they are shown in the employ of the Rural District Council, one imagines that the modern equivalent would probably be that of 'waste-recycler'. The census still shows that many people were domestic servants, although a proportion of these were older daughters who had stayed at home to help look after their parents and family. One striking feature is the large number of doctors or physicians listed for such a relatively small population.

For a while it seemed like the Robinson family dream for the development of Lee-on-the-Solent as a residential seaside resort to challenge the likes of Bournemouth and Southsea for wealthy Victorian families was gradually becoming realised. However, the entrepreneurial spirit of the times would be quenched within the next three years as first the threat and then the eventual state of war arrived in Europe. The outbreak of the Great War on 28 July 1914 largely caused a moratorium on the construction of new dwellings. Many of the young men in the local area heeded the call that their Country needed them and many did not return, as the remembrance memorial near the site of the former Lee Tower bears a too tragic testimony.

The Great War not only took its toll on the population of Lee, but also on the town itself. Prior to 1914, a number of roads and private residences had been established to the west of Richmond Road and Kings Road. This area, which had been the subject of auction sales in the early part of that century, included Grenville Road, Marlborough Road, Cowes Road, Tennyson Road and Westcliff Road. With the arrival of the RNAS/RAF in Lee, all these roads, together with the buildings around them and almost 20 substantial private residences, were requisitioned and became part of the air base. Those roads and many, but by no means all, of those properties would never again form part of the civilian town.

The extensive social changes experienced nationally between the wars were also reflected within Lee-on-the-Solent. Motor transport rapidly became the dominant force and we have seen how the railway soon closed. The emphasis and types of occupation had changed beyond all recognition from the old days before the Great War. The old ways of agriculture, which had lasted for centuries up to that time, were barely evident in the area and those farms which had managed to survive were soon swept away. Melville (or Milville) Farm and Swaggs Farm both fell victim to the airfield expansion of the 1930s and 1940s. Court Barn Farm was engulfed in the housing development which pushed ever northwards, although the farmhouse (which is now a Grade II listed building) survives as the Conservative Club, and the farm's splendid barn is preserved as one of the exhibits at the Weald and Downland Open Air Museum in Singleton, West Sussex. Shoot Farmhouse remains, but has been a private residence for many years since the farm ceased.

During this time, many more residential properties were established in the town, although a substantial number of them still had no mains drainage but relied on septic tanks in the back garden. Many homes still required water to be pumped up by hand from a well and both lighting and cooking was done by gas, as there was no electricity available.

In 1930, the town was also the subject of some important local political changes. Under the Ministry of Health Provisional Order Confirmation (Gosport Extension) Act 1930, Lee was finally separated from the parish of Crofton, of which it had long been part up to that time, and became a new parish but within the area and control of the Borough of Gosport. Local elections were held on 19 March 1930 for the first local councillors to represent the three seats created in the new Lee ward: the successful candidates were Arthur Sillitoe, pharmacist, Montague Gibbs, builder, and Trevor Tatham, architect. The official transfer to Gosport took place on Tuesday, 1 April 1930 and was marked by a civic ceremony and procession which commenced at Thorngate Halls.

During the 1930s the Art Deco craze which swept across Europe was in evidence locally in the design of the Lee Tower, some of the houses on the western side of Milvil Road and Marine Court Mansions in Marine Parade West (a life-size replica of part of these shops is one of the exhibits at the Milestones Living History Museum in Basingstoke). At this time, the town was able to boast four garages, two public houses, five hotels, two guesthouses and four banks. It is sobering to reflect upon how many of these remain.

At the end of the 1940s there were still gas lamps in the streets, but they were few and far between. Although they were not lit during the war, a man came round to light them at dusk after the War. There was one on the corner of Anglesea Road and Gosport Road, and another at the junction of Brickland Terrace and Wootton Road. At that time, many roads in the Elmore end of Lee were unadopted – in other words, not made up. They were not covered with tarmac, and were often full of potholes, particularly in Anglesea Road, Wootton Road, and Gosport Road as far as Cross Road and, when it rained, the puddles made it almost impossible to walk 'dry shod' along these roads.

The inter-war years were also the times when day-trippers would flock to Lee to go to the beach, the Tower or the swimming pool. While Victorians were, of course, no strangers to the beach, by the time the 1930s arrived there was not only greater freedom of travel but also many of the social strictures had evaporated and people felt a greater sense of freedom. Hence their ability, for example, to travel for miles to Lee-on-the-Solent to seek out a good spot for a picnic and enjoy the spectacle of the air displays or the events taking place on the Solent. These years also saw other great changes and innovations in social life, particularly in music, dance and cinema. Once again, the town was able to both embrace and encourage these through the new facilities offered at the Tower Complex.

History was, of course, to repeat itself in 1939 when the outbreak of the Second World War saw further sacrifices by the fighting men and women and the civilians of Lee. Once again the town experienced some widespread changes under the defence regulations with some 65 separate areas being requisitioned, including over 50 private residential and business properties.

After the War, the building programme seen nationally also occurred in Lee and the town grew considerably in the following decades. Unable to expand west because of the airbase, south because of the sea, and east because of Browndown, the town started to push further and further northwards. Private, council, military and 'prefab' housing transformed both the size and character of the town. New roads were constructed and existing ones expanded to deal with this growth. The town remained popular for day-trippers and locals alike and an expansion of dedicated, as opposed to casual, car-parking was undertaken. Outsiders did not tend to stay, however, and eventually all five hotels that had flourished together in earlier years closed their doors with the result that, today, no hotel accommodation is available, although various guesthouses thrive.

With increases in population, wealth and income and the desire for comfort and enjoyment, it was perhaps inevitable that many of the old villas, especially those along Marine Parade, would eventually become victims of demolition contractors and be replaced with new apartment blocks in which many more people could enjoy the views and facilities on offer. Over recent years, there has been an increase in the proportion of elderly residents within the town and this, linked with the value of the 'grey pound', has encouraged developers to establish a number of sheltered housing complexes both along the seafront and in the High Street.

The defence of the realm has always been driven by political and financial factors and so it is no surprise that, with a large military presence, Lee-on-the-Solent has witnessed many changes. Whereas in years past the presence of naval personnel was very much an inherent part of the town community and society, the run down and ultimate closure of HMS Daedalus has meant that Lee has had to adapt to the loss of this part of its life. Actually, it seems to have coped very well.

The brand new town of the 1880s has certainly come of age and, like many others, it has changed much over the years. Whilst the entrepreneurial Robinsons might have welcomed the expansion and popularity of the resort, they could never have envisaged how the area would develop. Some people will no doubt lament many of the changes which have occurred, but nowhere can be frozen in time and it is always easy to look back through rose-tinted spectacles. There have been good times and there have been bad times. The original dreams and aspirations of the Robinsons in attempting to create a successful seaside resort were never realised, but such failure was down to the vast changes witnessed in the very late years of the nineteenth century and in the early part of the twentieth century rather than any inherent shortcoming on their part. Instead, what they did create in the end was a popular residential town. Today, many of its residents regularly voice their appreciation of the town and feel themselves fortunate to live in it, and it still has much to offer...and, when all is said and done, it is still good to have an opportunity of **Exploring the History of Lee-on-the-Solent**.

APPENDICES

Appendix 1
Doomsday Book Entries

The Doomsday Book of 1086, which could be described as the national census and stocktaking account of the conquering Normans, gives an idea of the relative size and importance of the settlements existing in our area at that time. The entries, which have been simplified, for the area are:-

Alverstoke

50 households (very large).

48 villagers. 2 smallholders.

15 ploughlands. 16 men's plough teams.

Crofton

17 households (medium).

11 villagers. 2 smallholders. 4 slaves.

5 ploughlands. 1 lord's plough team. 4.5 men's plough teams.

Other resources: Meadow 24 acres. Woodland 5 swine render.

1 mill, 1 fishery. 2 salthouses. 1 church.

Meon

2 households (very small).

2 villagers.

1 ploughland.

Other resources: Woodland 2 acres.

Rowner

14 households (medium).

10 villagers. 2 smallholders. 2 slaves.

4 ploughlands. 1.5 lord's plough teams. 2.5 men's plough teams.

Other resources: Meadow 1 acres. Woodland 4 swine render.

Stubbington

9 households (quite small).

5 villagers. 4 smallholders.

3 ploughlands. 1 lord's plough team. 2 men's plough teams.

Other resources: Meadow 2 acres.

Titchfield

33 households (quite large).

16 villagers. 13 smallholders. 4 slaves.

15 ploughlands. 0.3 lord's plough teams. 9 men's plough teams.

Other resources: Meadow 14 acres. 2 mills.

With the exception of Alverstoke (which came under Meonstoke), all of these settlements were included in the 'hundred' of Titchfield. Lee was not recorded as a separate community at that time.

In the terms used in the Doomsday Book a 'hundred' was one of the units of land into which a Shire (county) was divided. It was originally introduced by the Saxons between 613 and 1017. Each hundred had enough land to sustain approximately 100 households and may also have referred to an area with the liability of providing a hundred men under arms should the need arise. In the traditional Germanic system this unit was used for administrative and judicial as well as military purposes. Hundreds formed the administrative units between the parish and the county and remained in place until the introduction of districts by the Local Government Act, 1894.

Within each hundred there was a meeting place where the men discussed local issues and judicial trials were held and the name of the hundred was normally that of its meeting-place. Although a shire-reeve (sheriff) had control of the shire, of which a hundred formed part, hundred boundaries were independent of both parish and county boundaries, all of which tended to complicate matters. As the country was being divided into counties when the Doomsday Book was being compiled and the system of hundreds was not very rigid, it frequently resulted in lists differing as to how many hundreds there were in a county.

For judicial purposes there were hundred courts, and the administration of law and keeping of the peace progressively became the principal function of the hundred. Except for especially serious crimes, the hundred was under the jurisdiction of the crown and the chief magistrate would be a sheriff. Many hundreds, however, were in private hands, with the lordship of the hundred being attached to the principal manor of the area. Where a hundred was under a lord, a steward, the chief official of the Lord of the Manor, was appointed in place of a sheriff. The importance of the hundred courts declined from the seventeenth century, and most of their powers were removed with the establishment of county courts in 1867.

When the Doomsday Book was compiled, the hundred was important as a unit for assessing and gathering taxes as well as for raising men for the citizen army. Hundreds were divided into tithings, which contained ten households.

A 'ploughland' was the unit of tax assessment based on the area one ox might till in a single annual season (about 15 acres). It was a very variable unit and indicated the profitability of the land but had no fixed relationship to its area. This is because many of the units of measurement were rather vague. For example, a furlong or length of a medieval field was very variable, as it was usual for horses to take a short rest at the end of the furrow before turning in to the next furrow. The heavier the soil, the harder the horses had to work, and so the less time between rests. In some cases this led to shorter furrows or furlongs giving rise to local variations in furlong length. These variations remained for some eight hundred years until the advent of the railways when a standard measurement became essential. The radius of curvature of a track was measured in chains, where one chain is equal to one tenth of a furlong, that is 22 yards *[20m]*. For measurement of smaller distances there were 100 links to a chain, making a link approximately 8 inches *[20cm]*. The names for these measurements derive from the fact that distances were actually measured with real links and chains made of metal.

A rod, pole or perch (believed to have derived its name from the typical length of a stick used in mediaeval times to prod the ox pulling the plough), was a length equal to 5½ yards *[5m]*. The furlong was standardised to be exactly 40 rods long, and the acre which was initially defined as the amount of land tillable by one man behind one ox in one day was standardised as a furlong in length and four rods wide (160 square rods or roods) which equals 4840 sq yards.

Appendix 2
Town Time Line

Principal dates and events

1883   The Robinson family acquires over 264 acres and immediately starts laying out streets and dividing the land into plots for sale at public auctions

1884   The Victoria Hotel, developed from an old farmhouse, opens for business

First public auction selling plots of land (3 September)

1885   Foundation stone of pier laid (July)

Brick making starts

1888   Pier opens (3 April)

1890   Foundation ceremony of railway (22 October)

1891   Lee Waterworks Company formed

1894   Original sea wall constructed

Railway opens (31 March)

St Faith's temporary church building established

1897   Methodist Church opens

1908   County Primary School opens (28 September)

Lee Lawn Tennis Club founded

1916   St John's temporary church building established

1917   HM Naval Seaplane School opens (30 July). Various properties requisitioned by the Admiralty

1926   Inn-by-the-Sea opens (19 July)

1929   Huge crowds amass to witness The Schneider Trophy Competition (7 September)

1930   Lee becomes part of Borough of Gosport (1 April)

The famous *R100* airship passes over the town on a return test-flight to the Channel Islands (26 July)

1931   Railway closes for passenger traffic (1 January)

Swimming pool constructed

Air base expanded including large building programme

Huge crowds amass to witness the return of The Schneider Trophy Competition off shore (13 September)

1932   Pier damaged by fire (19 June)

1933   New St Faith's Church opens and old tin church removed

1935   Railway closes for goods traffic (30 September)

Tower complex opens (26 December)

1937   Public Library opens in High Street (November)

1939   Railway track removed

Various properties requisitioned by the Admiralty

1940   Pier breached as part of defence measures (July)

King George VI visits HMS Daedalus (July)

First air raid (16 August)

1944   Thousands of troops embark from Lee on D-Day invasion (6 June)

1946   Programme of building prefabricated housing

1949   Swimming pool closes and is converted into children's paddling pools

1951   Housing development on northern edge of town

1952   The Queen makes a royal visit (21 November)

1953   The Queen makes a second royal visit and presents the Colours at HMS Daedalus (30 July)

1958   Remains of pier demolished

1959   Work starts on further sea defences including extension of sea wall

1963   Princess Marina, Duchess of Kent, visits HMS Daedalus to open a new purpose-built accommodation block for female naval ratings (18 July)

1971   Tower complex demolished

1976/7 Housing development on northern edge of town

1980   New St John's Church opens and old asbestos hut removed

        Princess Anne visits WRNS at HMS Daedalus (24 June)

1982   Community Centre opens (29 March)

1985/6 Housing development on northern edge of town

        Prince Andrew visits HMS *Daedalus* for Fleet Air Arm Reunion
        (September)

1996   HMS *Daedalus* closes

1996/7 Work to build up beach levels

2003   Protest marches and rallies held in the town against the
        establishment of an immigration centre

2005/6 Housing development on eastern edge of town

2006   Largest civilian peacetime evacuation to allow bomb disposal
        at the airfield.

Appendix 3
Street and Road Names

It is often possible to find the derivation of the names given to those streets and roads laid out by the Robinson family during the initial development of Lee-on-the-Solent:

Anglesea Road after 'Anglesea Ville' often used as a variation of the name 'Anglesey Ville', a former name for the local area (especially Crescent Road and St Marks Road, Gosport). This was named after Henry William Paget, 1st Marquess of Anglesey who is widely considered to have laid the foundation stone of the earliest building in that area (Uxbridge House) in 1826. However 104 years later, a letter was found in an old writing desk written by the Marquess apologising for being unable to attend the official ceremony due to a sudden illness and deputising his son, the Earl of Uxbridge, to attend in his stead. A very early plan prepared by the Lee-on-the-Solent Estates Company in 1884 shows that this road was originally to have been at a different angle from that which was eventually built and that the original name proposed for it was Fareham Road.

Beach Road after the fact that it ran down directly onto the beach. Originally it continued on the south side of Marine Parade East where there was a boat-house located immediately north of the railway line. A very early plan prepared by the Lee-on-the-Solent Estates Company in 1884 shows it was originally intended that that road would extend north of the High Street to link up with what is now Lulworth Road.

Britten Road after Lee Britten, one of the old manors in the area.

Broom Way after Broom House and Broom House Farm, which were agricultural properties in this area in the early days of the development. They were situated on the western side of the current site of Broom Way and their location is now covered by the eastern edge of the airfield.

Cambridge Road possibly after the university which Charles Edmund Robinson attended and graduated from with a Master of Arts degree (Trinity College). He remained very fond of the establishment.

Clanwilliam Road after Elizabeth Henrietta Meade, the Countess of Clanwilliam. She was a local dignitary who was married to Admiral Richard James Meade, 4th Earl of Clanwilliam and Naval Commander in Chief of Portsmouth. The Countess was chief magistrate of the Borough of Portsmouth and performed the opening ceremony of the Lee-on-the-Solent Railway in May 1894. The road was named and laid out around 1895, slightly later than most of the others. Its course was straight across the middle of the former cricket field which had been established at the very beginning of the development.

Court Road after Court Farm, one of the pre-development farms that had existed in the area.

Cross Road Although the origin of the name is uncertain, a very early plan prepared by the Lee-on-the-Solent Estates Company in 1884 shows that the original name proposed for this road was Albert Road and that it was to have extended in a continuous straight line beyond the other side of what is now Raynes Road.

Elmore Road after the name of the local area of this part of Lee. A very early plan prepared by the Lee-on-the-Solent estates Company in 1884 shows that the original name proposed for this road was Elmore Place.

Flower Buildings after Frederick R Flower, local estate agent, who had his office in the building. A prominent local figure, he was a member of Fareham UDC, parish councillor, school manager and member of the Board of Guardians (see Chapter 8).

Inverkip Close after 'Inverkip', a large private residence which was established on the site in the early 1900s. It was requisitioned in the Great War and on 25 March 1943 was transferred by the War Department for use as RNAS accommodation before being demolished to make way for the present housing development.

King's Road Although the origin of the name is uncertain, a very early plan prepared by the Lee-on-the-Solent Estates Company in 1884 shows that the original name proposed for this road was York Place.

Lulworth Road after the area in Dorset close to Sir John Charles Robinson's home. A very early plan prepared by the Lee-on-the-Solent Estates Company in 1884 shows that the original name proposed for this road and also for the northern portion of Studland Road was Osborne Place.

Manor Way after the manor house which used to exist in the area. A very early plan prepared by the Lee-on-the-Solent Estates Company in 1884 shows that the original name proposed for the northern portion of this road was Avenue Road.

Milvil Road after the early hamlet, Millville, which was located further north along it in the pre-development days.

Newton Place after the maiden name of Sir John Charles Robinson's wife, Lady Marian. Newton Manor was also the name of his home in Swanage, Dorset. Charles Edmund Robinson also made his surname into the double-barrelled form of Newton-Robinson in 1889. This was one of the very earliest roads to be built on the estate.

Norwich Place after the city in which Lady Marian Robinson had been born and brought up.

Nottingham Place after the city in which Sir John Charles Robinson had been born, brought up and educated.

Osborne Road after Osborne House, Queen Victoria's residence on the Isle of Wight with which the road is aligned.

Petrie Road after Alfred Ernest Petrie, one of the active participants in the early development of the town. He was a director of the Lee-on-the-Solent Pier Company from the mid 1880s. The road was named and laid out in the late 1890s, slightly later than most of the others.

Pier Street after the fact that it ran down to the location of the old wooden jetty. Originally it was part of Manor Way and then briefly called Pier Road.

Portsmouth Road clearly named after the nearby city but a very early plan prepared by the Lee-on-the-Solent estates Company in 1884 shows that the original name proposed for this road was Browndown Road after the Common nearby.

Raynes Road after Thomas Andrew Raynes of Ventnor, auctioneer, who was one of the active participants in the early development of the town. He was a director of the Lee-on-the-Solent Pier Company from the mid 1880s and also owned some of the land on which the Methodist Church was later built. A very early plan prepared by the Lee-on-the-Solent Estates Company in 1884 shows that the original name proposed for this road was Portsmouth Road.

Ryde Place after the town of Ryde on the Isle of Wight with which it is roughly aligned.

Seymour Road although the origin of the name is uncertain, a very early plan prepared by the Lee-on-the-Solent Estates Company in 1884 shows that the original name proposed for this road was Albany Road.

Skipper Way after Gladys May Skipper (1900-1985), a prominent and active member of the local community, who served as a town councillor for over twenty years and later became an honorary Alderman (see Chapter 8).

Studland Road after the area in Dorset close to Sir John Charles Robinson's home. A very early plan prepared by the Lee-on-the-Solent Estates Company in 1884 shows that the original name proposed for the northern portion of this road and also for Lulworth Road was Osborne Place.

Swanage Road after the location of Sir John Charles Robinson's beloved home, Newton Manor, in Swanage, Dorset.

Victoria Square after Queen Victoria, the reigning monarch at the time the town was first laid out and in whose employ Sir

John Charles Robinson held the post of Crown Surveyor of Pictures. The southern corner of the square points directly along Osborne Road to the Queen Victoria's residence at Osborne House on the Isle of Wight.

Wootton Road after the location on the Isle of Wight with which it is roughly aligned.

Appendix 4
The War Dead
whose names appear on the Lee-on-the-Solent War Memorial

THE GREAT WAR

William Herbert Adams, Private in the Royal Berkshire Regiment, died 16 June 1917, buried at St Mary's Churchyard, Hook, Hampshire. He lived at Titchfield and later at Hook.

William Ayling (19), Private in the Hampshire Regiment, died 9 July 1915, commemorated on the Ypres (Menin Gate) Memorial, Belgium. He lived at Stubbington Lane, Fareham.

Edwin Bailey (20), Private in the Hampshire Regiment, died 15 September 1916, commemorated on the Thiepval Memorial, Somme, France. He lived at Marks Road, Stubbington.

Reuben George Barnard (32), Ship's Steward aboard *HMS Hogue*, died 22 September 1914, commemorated on the Chatham Naval Memorial.

Sydney Claude Hamilton Begbie (21), Lieutenant in the RAF, died 22 April 1918, buried at Lille Southern Cemetery, France. He lived at Hill Head.

William Bird (32), Sergeant in the Canadian Signal Corps (Signal Training Depot), died 19 December 1916, buried at Kingston (Cataraqui) Cemetery, Ontario, Canada. He was brought up in Hill Head and his parents continued to live there.

Henry Gardiner Burridge (24), Lieutenant in the 107th Indian Pioneers, died 19 November 1914, buried at Bethune Town Cemetery, Pas de Calais, France.

Frederick George Burch (19), Private in the Hampshire Regiment, died 15 September 1916, buried at Bulls Road Cemetery, Flers, Somme, France. He lived at 'Tankerton House', Lee-on-the-Solent.

Harold Royston Clark (22), Private in the Royal Sussex Regiment, died 10 April 1916, buried at Fareham Cemetery. He lived at Stubbington.

Edward John Coffin (34), Private in the Royal Marine Light Infantry, *HMS Viknor*, died 13 January 1915, commemorated on the Portsmouth Naval Memorial. He lived at Gosport Road, Lee-on-the-Solent.

A Cook – [no details identified].

W Cook – [no details identified].

Llewellyn Godfrey Mortimer Egremont (34), Private in the Hampshire Regiment, died 12 October 1917, buried at the Cairo War Memorial Cemetery, Egypt. He lived at 'Llanstephen', Lee-on-the-Solent.

Archibald Courtenay Hayes Foster (28), Lieutenant in the Hampshire Regiment attached to the King's African Rifles, died 18 September 1914, commemorated on the Nairobi British and Indian Memorial, Nairobi, Kenya. He lived at Stubbington. Brother of William John Foster.

William John Foster (30), Lieutenant Commander aboard *HM Submarine E6*, died 26 December 1915, commemorated on the Portsmouth Naval Memorial. His parents lived at Stubbington. Brother of Archibald Courtenay Hayes Foster.

Thomas John Franklin (23), Private in the Hampshire Regiment, died 29 April 1915, commemorated on the Ypres (Menin Gate) Memorial, Belgium. He was a native of Stubbington.

T J Goodall – [no details identified].

Sidney Henry Gover (30), Mechanician aboard *HMS Black Prince*, died 31 May 1916 when she was sunk at the Battle of Jutland, commemorated on the Portsmouth Naval Memorial. His family lived at High Street, Lee-on-the-Solent.

Robert Crosby Halahan (31), Lieutenant Commander aboard *HM Submarine E18*, died 11 June 1916, commemorated on the Portsmouth Naval Memorial. He lived at Stubbington.

Reginald Vile Hallett (23), Gunner in the Royal Field Artillery, died 12 March 1919, buried at Crofton (Holy Rood) Old Churchyard. He lived at The Red Lion, Stubbington.

Charles Ronald Harris (21), Sapper in the Royal Engineers (1st/6th Hants Electric Light Company), died 6 February 1918, buried at Gosport (Ann's Hill) Cemetery. He lived at Cambridge Road, Lee-on-the-Solent.

George Henry Harrison (34), Private in the Devonshire Regiment, died 5 January 1917, buried at Crofton (Holy Rood) Old Churchyard. He lived at Stubbington.

H Harrison – [no details identified].

George Alfred Hayward (31), Stoker 1st Class aboard *HMS Victory*, died 2 November 1918, buried at Haslar Royal Naval Cemetery. He lived at Brickfield Cottages, Lee-on-the-Solent.

W Hayward – [no details identified].

William E Hewes (26), Bombardier in the Royal Garrison Artillery, died 30 August 1917, buried in the Duhallow ADS Cemetery, Belgium. He lived at Gosport Road, Lee-on-the-Solent.

James Hellyer, Leading Stoker aboard *HMS Good Hope*, died 1 November 1914, commemorated on the Portsmouth Naval Memorial.

William Oliver Fitzer Judd (21), Private in the North Staffordshire Regiment, died 17t January 1918, buried at the Rocquigny-Equancourt Road British Cemetery, Somme, France. He lived at Stubbington.

Nicholas Mainger King (39) Stoker in the RN Reserve aboard *HMS Hawke*, died 15 October 1914, commemorated on the Chatham Naval Memorial.

C Locke – [no details identified].

Auriol Ernest Eric Lowry (25), Lieutenant Colonel in the West Yorkshire Regiment (Prince of Wales's Own), died

23 September 1918, buried at La Targette British Cemetery, Neuville-St Vaast, France. Awarded DSO, MC and Croix de Guerre de Palme. He lived at 'Ryde View', Lee-on-the-Solent and later at Manor Way, Lee-on-the-Solent. Brother of Cyril John Patrick Lowry and William Augustine Harper Lowry.

Cyril John Patrick Lowry (20), Captain in the West Yorkshire Regiment (Prince of Wales's Own), died 25 March 1918 commemorated on the Pozieres Memorial, Somme, France. He lived at 'Ryde View', Lee-on-the-Solent and later at Manor Way, Lee-on-the-Solent. Brother of Auriol Ernest Eric Lowry and William Augustine Harper Lowry.

William Augustine Harper Lowry (25), Second Lieutenant in the Indian Army Reserve of Officers attached to 14th King George's Own Ferozepore Sikhs, died at Gallipoli on 4 June 1915, commemorated on the Helles Memorial, Turkey. Mentioned in dispatches. He lived at 'Ryde View', Lee-on-the-Solent and later at Manor Way, Lee-on-the-Solent. Brother of Auriol Ernest Eric Lowry and Cyril John Patrick Lowry.

Percy Luff (35), Sergeant in the RAF 5th Balloon Section, died 28 May 1918, buried at Mendinghem Military Cemetery, Belgium. He lived at Petrie Road and later at Gosport Road, Lee-on-the-Solent.

Leofwin Collings Fellowes Lukis (19), Second Lieutenant in the Royal Flying Corps and Essex Regiment, died 6 January 1917, buried at St Ouen Communal Cemetery, Somme, France.

Thomas Marchant (17), Signal Boy aboard *HMS Emperor of India*, died 21 February 1919, buried at Haslar Royal Naval Cemetery. He lived at Hill Head.

H C Mead – [no details identified].

John Mitchell (21), Private in the Hampshire Regiment, died 4 November 1917, buried at Monchy British Cemetery, Monchy-le-Preux, France. He lived at Stubbington.

E Morris – [no details identified].

P J Morris – [no details identified].

Sidney Muckett (21), Private in the Hampshire Regiment, died 20 September 1917, commemorated on the Tyne Cot Memorial, Belgium. He lived at Stubbington.

Frederick James New (19), Private in the Hampshire Regiment, died 24 February 1917, commemorated on the Basra Memorial, Iraq. He lived at Gosport Road, Lee-on-the-Solent.

Hedley John Newman (36), Gunner in the Royal Garrison Artillery, died 4 September 1917, buried at Coxyde Military Cemetery, Belgium. He lived at Gosport Road, Lee-on-the-Solent.

Connie Aubrey Newman (29), Engine Room Artificer 3rd Class aboard *HMS Good Hope*, died 1 November 1914, commemorated on the Portsmouth Naval Memorial.

Reginald Arthur Odell (25), Sergeant in the Hampshire Regiment, died 30 June 1916, commemorated on the Basra Memorial, Iraq. Mentioned in Dispatches. He lived at Hill Head. Brother of William James Odell.

William James Odell (29), Sergeant in the Hampshire Regiment, died 12 March 1918, commemorated on the Tehran Memorial, Iraq. He lived at Hill Head. Brother of Reginald Arthur Odell.

Eric Frank Packham (19), Second Lieutenant in the Army Services Corp attached to the Hampshire Regiment, died 1 November 1918, buried at Crofton (Holy Rood) Old Churchyard. He lived at Stubbington.

Douglas Stanley Pike (23), Rifleman in the King's Royal Rifle Corp., died 24 March 1918, buried in the Rosieres British Cemetery, Somme, France. He lived at Gosport Road, Lee-on-the-Solent.

James Redman (18), Private in the Hampshire Regiment, died 7 October 1916, commemorated on the Thiepval Memorial, Somme, France. He lived at Stubbington.

Arthur Rye (20), Private in the Hampshire Regiment, died 26 September 1917, commemorated on the Tyne Cot Memorial. Belgium. He lived at Hill Head.

W Smith – [no details identified].

Harry Stretch (37), Chief Stoker in the Royal Australian Navy aboard *HM Submarine AE1* (on loan from British Navy), died 14 September 1914, commemorated on the Plymouth Naval Memorial. He lived at Stubbington.

Herbert Charles Thick (32), Private in the Gloucestershire Regiment, died 5 November 1914, commemorated on the Ypres (Menin Gate) Memorial, Belgium. He lived at Gosport Road, Lee-on-the-Solent.

John Ellery Tizard (31), Assistant Paymaster aboard *HMS Good Hope*, died 1 November 1914, commemorated on the Portsmouth Naval Memorial.

Harold Tribbeck (21), Lance Corporal in the Royal Warwickshire Regiment, died 29 October 1918, buried at Crofton (Holy Rood) Old Churchyard. He lived at Stubbington.

William George Tutt-Harris (24), Private in the Hampshire Regiment, died 3 September 1916, commemorated on the Thiepval Memorial, Somme, France. His family lived at Stubbington.

A Ward – [no details identified].

Horace Vivian Ward (19), Rifleman in the King's Royal Rifle Corp, died 24 August 1917, commemorated on the Tyne Cot Memorial, Belgium. He lived at Seymour Road, Lee-on-the-Solent.

Charles Alfred Henry Warland (20), Private in the Queen's (Royal West Surrey Regiment), died 4 October 1917, commemorated on the Tyne Cot Memorial, Belgium. He lived at 'Canford', Lee-on-the-Solent.

Arthur Wells (40), Private in the Hampshire Regiment, died 7 October 1917, buried at the Agra Cantonment Cemetery, India, commemorated on the Madras 1914-1918 War Memorial, Chennai, India. He lived at Bricklands Terrace, Gosport Road, Lee-on-the-Solent. Brother of Matthias Wells.

Matthias Wells (32), Private in the Hampshire Regiment, died 3 September 1916, commemorated on the Thiepval Memorial, Somme, France. He lived at Gosport Road, Lee-on-the-Solent. Brother of Arthur Wells.

Frank Oliver Weyman (18) Cook 2nd Class aboard *HMS Black Prince*, died 31 March 1916 when she sank during the Battle of Jutland, commemorated on the Portsmouth Naval Memorial. He lived at Stubbington.

Harry Percy Wheeler (37), Private in the Norfolk Regiment, died 11 August 1917, commemorated on the Ypres (Menin Gate) Memorial, Belgium.

Harold Conrad Wise (31) Private in the Honourable Artillery Company, died 3 May 1917, commemorated on the Arras Memorial, Pas de Calais, France. He lived at 'Lulworth', Lee-on-the-Solent.

Charles Douglas Hamlyn Yonge (30), Private in the Canadian Infantry, died 17 August 1917, commemorated on the Vimy Memorial, France. He lived at Crofton.

SECOND WORLD WAR

Geoffrey Browning (24), Civilian, son of Beatrice Browning, died as a result of his injuries on 16 August 1940 at Gosport War Memorial Hospital, buried at Ann's Hill Cemetery, Gosport. His family were bakers in High Street, Lee-on-the-Solent.

William Edward Buck (24), Driver in the Royal Army Services Corps, died 20 March 1940, buried at Ramleh War Cemetery, Israel and Palestine.

Lewis Thomas George Clark (32), Civilian, died 26 March 1941 at South-Western Tar Distilleries, buried at New Forest Rural District Cemetery.

Hubert Edward Cook (30), Gunner in the Royal Horse Artillery, died 12 June 1942, commemorated on the Alamein Memorial, Egypt. He lived at Lee-on-the-Solent.

Berkeley Leonard Copland, (22) Engine Room Artificer 4th Class aboard *HMS Beverley*, died 11 April 1943 when she was sunk by a U-boat, commemorated on the Portsmouth Naval Memorial. He lived at Lee-on-the-Solent.

Charles Douglas Dimmick (29), Private in the Hampshire Regiment, died 22 April 1943, buried in the Massicault War Cemetery, Tunisia. He lived at Lee-on-the-Solent.

Sidney Harry Dimmick (21), Driver in the Royal Engineers, died between 28 May 1940 and 28 June 1940, buried at Dunkirk Town Cemetery, France.

Albert Charles Drayson (21), Able Seaman aboard French torpedo boat *Branlebas* (which the British had captured off Portsmouth on 3 July 1940), died 14 December 1940 when she foundered in a storm off Dartmouth, commemorated on the Portsmouth Naval Memorial. His family lived at 63 Seymour Road, Lee-on-the-Solent.

Charles Gentry Evans (39), Chief Petty Officer aboard *HMS Acheron*, died 17 December 1940 when she struck a mine and sank off the Isle of Wight, commemorated on the Portsmouth Naval Memorial.

Victor Bowring Field (24), Flying Officer in the RAF, died 20 August 1943, commemorated on the Alamein Memorial, Egypt. His family lived at 15 Raynes Road, Lee-on-the-Solent.

Cyril Iggo Fitch (24), Engine Room Artificer 3rd Class aboard *HMS Welshman* (an Abdiel class minelayer), died 1 February 1943 when she was sunk by a U-boat east of Tobruk, commemorated on the Chatham Naval Memorial. Mentioned in despatches. His family lived at Victoria Square, Lee-on-the-Solent. Brother of Jack Dunning Fitch.

Jack Dunning Fitch (27), Flight Sergeant in the RAF, died 27 December 1942, commemorated on the Runnymede

Memorial, Surrey. His family lived at Victoria Square, Lee-on-the-Solent. Brother of Cyril Iggo Fitch.

Cecil Leonard Albert Grout (15), Civilian, died 16 August 1940, buried at Ann's Hill Cemetery, Gosport. His family lived at 22 Elmore Avenue, Lee-on-the-Solent.

Leo Henry Hawkins, (27) Sergeant in the Royal Air Force Volunteer Reserve, died 15 October 1942, buried in Rowner (St Mary) Churchyard, Gosport. He lived at Lee-on-the-Solent.

Douglas Egbert Hunter BA (60), Civilian, Vicar of St. Faith's Church, Lee-on-the-Solent, injured at the vicarage on 16 May 1944 and died later the same day at the War Memorial Hospital, Gosport. His ashes are interred near the south door of St Faith's Church.

Samuel Gourley Nixon (20), Sapper in the Royal Engineers, died 3 June 1940, commemorated on the Dukirk Memorial, France. His family lived at Lee-on-the-Solent.

Norman Edwin Philbrick (22), Sergeant in the Royal Air Force Volunteer Reserve, died 16 July 1943, commemorated on the Malta Memorial, Malta. His family lived at 1 Grove Cottages, Grove Road, Lee-on-the-Solent.

Charles Henry Roberts (23), Able Seaman aboard *HMS Arrow*, died 4 August 1943 when she was set on fire at Algiers harbour by an explosion on board the merchant ship *SS Fort La Montee*, commemorated on the Portsmouth Naval Memorial. His family lived at Lee-on-the-Solent.

William Miles Smart (32) Petty Officer aboard *HMS Victor*, died 23 April 1943, buried at Haslar Royal Naval Cemetery. His family lived at 49 Seymour Road, Lee-on-the-Solent.

Roy Albert Wilfred Wilkinson (25), Sergeant (Air Gunner) in the RAF, died 16 July 1943, buried at the Milan War Cemetery, Italy. He lived at Lee-on-the-Solent.

These two names were added to the War Memorial later:

P Bryant – [no details identified].

D R Briggs – [no details identified].

One casualty whose name does not appear on the War Memorial is **William Denzil Livock** (21), Pilot Officer RAF Volunteer Reserve, died during flying operations on 21 December 1944, commemorated on the Runnymede Memorial. He was the son of Group Captain G E Livock and Mrs F Livock who lived at Lee-on-the-Solent.

SECOND WORLD WAR – The ten Wrens who were killed

Although their names are not commemorated on the Lee-on-the-Solent War Memorial it seems appropriate that details of the ten members of the WRNS who were killed on the night of 23 November 1940 at Mansfield House (see Chapter 19) are included here. They were:

Rosa May Armstrong (37), Wren (writer), buried at Haslar Royal Naval Cemetery.

Joyce Millicent Bennett (19) from Dorking in Surrey, Wren, buried at Dorking Cemetery.

Mona Violet Black (23) from Cheshire, Wren (writer), buried at Haslar Royal Naval Cemetery.

Winnie Blackett (19) from Thrybergh near Rotherham, Wren, buried at Moorgate Cemetery, Rotherham.

Vera Margaret Cowell (also Cowle) (18), Wren (steward), buried at Haslar Royal Naval Cemetery.

Nellie Gregory (32) from Cheshire, Leading Wren (leading steward), buried at Haslar Royal Naval Cemetery.

Beryl Melita Northfield (19) from Coulsden in Surrey, Wren, buried at Haslar Royal Naval Cemetery.

Hilda Pearson (26) from Plymouth in Devon, Leading Wren (leading writer), buried at Haslar Royal Naval Cemetery.

Norah Kathleen Reynolds (23) from Eastbourne in East Sussex, Wren (cook), buried at Haslar Royal Naval Cemetery.

Dorothy Margaret Wardell (22) from Yorkshire, Wren, buried at Haslar Royal Naval Cemetery.

Appendix 5
The Robinson Family's Other Development Projects

Although the following summaries are not part of the history of Lee-on-the-Solent, and therefore have no place in the main part of this account, they are appended in the hope that they may be of interest in illustrating the other projects pursued by the Robinsons before, during and after the time that they were active in Lee.

Swanage, Dorset

The second half of the nineteenth century saw a major expansion and redevelopment of Swanage. The men who were largely instrumental in these changes were John Robinson (who had moved to the town in 1872), John Mowlem (who had been born in the town and returned to it on his retirement in 1844 having made his fortune as a building contractor in London) and Mowlem's nephew, George Burt (who had worked with his uncle in the family firm and lived at the rather grand Purbeck House in the High Street). These three between them acquired large parts of the town and started to develop it into a successful seaside resort.

Mowlem constructed public buildings, monuments, and roads and developed a residential area in the northern part of the town. Burt is famous for bringing to the town many architectural features from London and re-erecting them in Swanage. He helped to provide water and gas supplies and also embarked on a grand scheme for the development of the Durlston Park Estate. Building progress was very slow, however, because this land was on a steep gradient. The only parts to be built were Park Road, Grosvenor Road, Durlston Road and Peveril Road together with a few terraces.

Initially John Robinson and George Burt were on friendly terms. Before he moved to Newton Manor, Robinson lived at 'St Aldhelm's' in Park Road on part of Burt's development. Actually the property was built above some old quarry workings and during the 1890s, some years after Robinson had moved out, it collapsed completely although, fortunately, without any loss of life.

In 1875 John Robinson bought a large parcel of land, known as Eightholds Manor, in the southern part of the town. This extended from the High Street right down to the Tilly Whim caves on the coast. It was one of several long plots of land, based on a pattern of land ownership dating from medieval times, which overlooked the coast and was located on the western side of the present-day Taunton Road. It also lay immediately west of George Burt's Durlston Estate.

Over the next few years, Robinson developed the northern section of this land and laid out new roads, Cluny Crescent, St Vaast Road, Stafford Road and Exeter Road, all being named after original ecclesiastical owners of the land. Later, a number of large seaside villas were built there. Robinson also established the row of shops known as King Alfred Terrace near George Burt's Town Hall in the High Street.

Although Robinson developed Bon Accord Road to link his new development with that of George Burt, the two men were by now in fact bitter rivals. There was much friction between them concerning the layout of the roads and Robinson always considered Burt to be an ignorant upstart. He even refused to use Burt's new water supply, preferring to build his own reservoir instead at the west end of the town near the Priest's Way. This supply also served Robinson's own property of Newton Manor.

It is interesting to note that many of the road names in John Robinson's part of the town are similar to those which he later used in Lee-on-the-Solent, for example Richmond Road, Osborne Road, Queens Road, Russell Avenue, Newton Road, York Terrace, Manor Road, Salisbury Road.

Tankerton, Kent

In 1890 the Tankerton Estate in Kent (which included Tankerton Tower and several farms) was on the market for sale. Charles Newton-

Robinson and his family saw potential for developing a resort in the location and in March of that year arranged to purchase the estate from Mr S W G Graystone for £22,000 *[£1,950,000]*. The Tankerton Estate Company was formed with the main purpose of developing the area and selling the land for building in order to create a "watering place for the best class".

After a slow start, the development expanded rapidly. A road was built through the grounds of the estate in 1891 and land was divided into building plots, which were gradually sold at a series of auctions commencing in the summer of that year. The Company soon ran into financial problems however and, in an effort to raise capital, the Tower and its then reduced area of grounds was mortgaged and rented out before the Company tried to sell it with a price tag of £10,000 *[£852,000]*. Eventually the Tower and its grounds were sold to Thomas Adams in 1897, but for only £3,350 *[£285,420]*. By 1914 the wider estate developed by the Company had some 300 houses constructed on it.

The Company was finally wound up in 1927 but building still proceeded and, by the outbreak of the Second World War, very few plots remained undeveloped.

Ravenscar, North Yorkshire

In 1895 Charles Newton-Robinson and his family arranged to purchase for £10,000 *[£928,000]* the entire area around the small village of Peak (which was later renamed Ravenscar in the early twentieth century). The plan was to develop the area as a resort to rival the likes of Scarborough, Whitby and even Blackpool. It was intended to sell off 1,500 plots of land for houses and to develop pleasure beaches with a view to the area thriving as a prosperous and large town. The Ravenscar Estate Company was formed and 300 men were employed to build roads, lay sewers and drains and to build houses. Catalogues were produced showing the plots that were for sale at the time and a local guidebook was published. Even special excursion trains were laid on to bring potential purchasers in from the cities of the West

Riding and the Midlands. The main feature of the resort was to be Marine Esplanade, comprising a long terrace of rather grand bed-and-breakfast properties.

The plan failed almost immediately. Few people put their money into the scheme and only a handful of plots were sold. The reasons for the failure are quite evident to anyone visiting the area today. While the location enjoys some truly spectacular views across the bay, the sea and weather conditions are unpredictable; the area being very exposed and often shrouded in mist from low cloud. At a height of some 630 feet [190m] above sea level, the route down to the sea is long, rocky and quite precarious as it suffers frequent erosion. Steps were carved into the side of the cliff, but it still proved to be a very difficult descent for the ladies of the time. All of these circumstances together with fact that, at the bottom of the cliff there is not even a proper beach but merely rocks and pools, meant that the project was destined for disaster.

The Company was wound up in 1913 (the year in which both Sir John Charles Robinson and Charles Newton-Robinson died) having built less than a dozen houses. Only one of the grand bed-and-breakfast houses planned to form the terrace along the Marine Esplanade was constructed and the rest of the resort was barely touched by the developers.

Today, old kerbstones and ornate manhole covers can be seen occasionally poking through the turf and it is little wonder that Ravenscar quickly earned the epithet of 'the resort that never was'.

Despite the failure of Charles Newton-Robinson's grand plan, he still seems to have retained pleasant memories of the area. Shortly before he died, he completed his last volume of poetry, entitled *Moods and Metres*, which was published posthumously. In that volume, at the end of a poem entitled *A Tyrol Valley*, he writes:

Deep would I draw one breath of Yorkshire free,
Half sea-whiff and half moorland heather, now,
From leagues of purple on that misty brow

Where Ravenscar juts out into the sea !
And dear are Dorset's windy downs to me,
Where the white cliffs of Swanage, like a prow,
Stem the unsleeping surge, and therebelow
Shelter the cosy townlet under lee !

Appendix 6
Maps and Plans

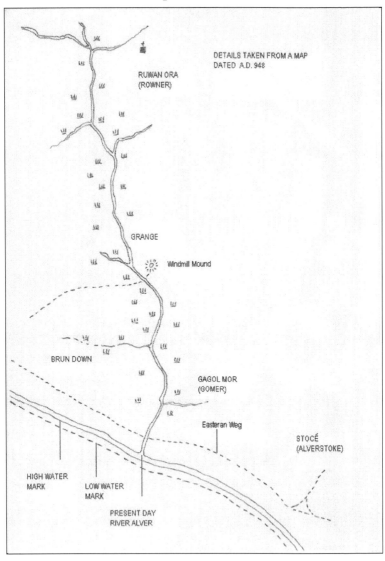

A plan showing the area around 948AD and the location of Windmill Mound

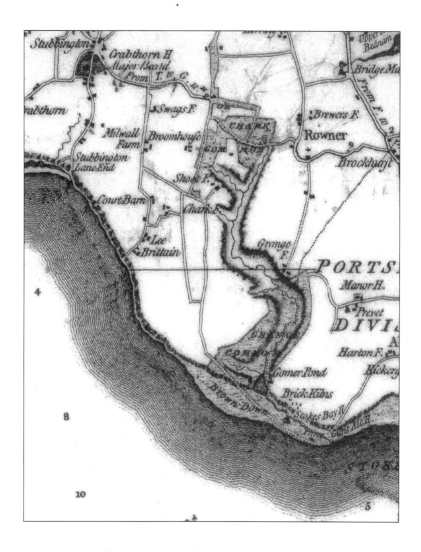

*Extract from a map dated 1791 showing the restricted access
then available to the area*

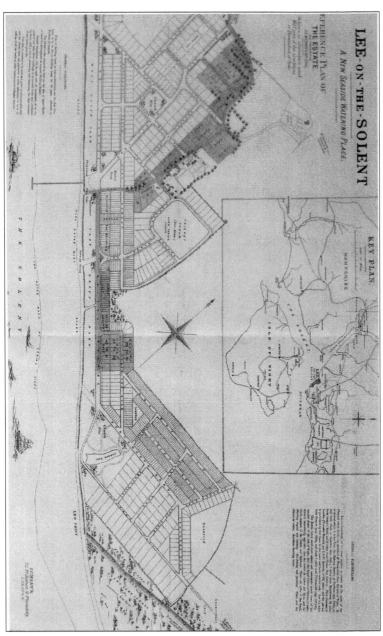

An early plan of the estate of Sir John Charles Robinson, 1884. The shaded
roads represent the only ones established at that time. The shaded plots
represent those that were put up for sale in the first two auctions

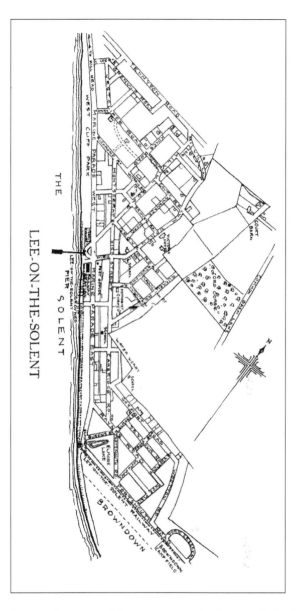

A plan showing the extent of the town in 1927 and particularly showing those roads in the west which were later requisitioned by the Admiralty and never returned to civilian use

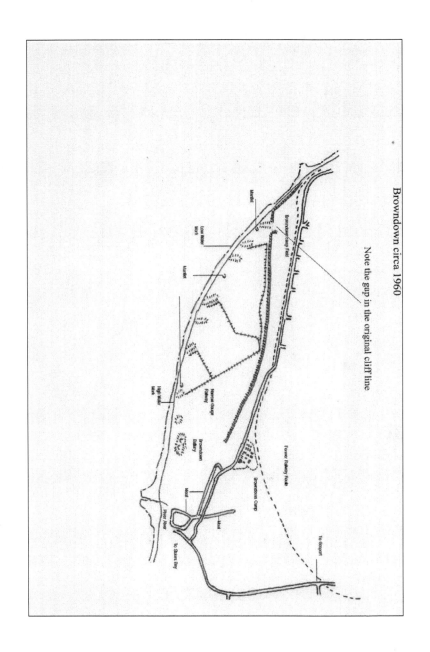

Browndown circa 1960

Note the gap in the original cliff line

Model

Low Water Mark

Mudlet

High Water Mark

Narrow Gauge Railway

Browndown Battery

Downstream Camp Field

Former Railway Route

Browndown Camp

Mud

Mud

River River

To States Bay

To Gosport

A plan showing the Browndown area in 1960 and the likely source of the material for used in the construction of the butts